DEADWOOD MURDER & MAYHEM

DEADWOOD MURDER & MAYHEM

DEBORAH CUYLE

THE History PRESS

Published by The History Press
An imprint of Arcadia Publishing
Charleston, SC
www.historypress.com

First published 2025

Manufactured in the United States

ISBN 9781467158404

Library of Congress Control Number: 2024951837

Notice: The information in this book is true and complete to the best of our knowledge. It is offered without guarantee on the part of the author or The History Press. The author and The History Press disclaim all liability in connection with the use of this book.

I dedicate this project to everyone who is as intrigued and passionate about Deadwood as I am! The mere word *Deadwood* conjures up all sorts of exciting thoughts—and the travel planning soon begins…

I am hoping to delight both locals and visitors to the Black Hills region with the stories in *Deadwood Murder & Mayhem*. A lot has changed in the town since its wild beginnings in 1875–76, when gold was discovered there. (Prospectors found gold earlier, in 1874, near present-day Custer, South Dakota, but the deposits turned out to be small and not much to get excited about.) It is interesting to note that when Deadwood was founded, it was essentially an illegal town, due to the fact that the land had already been granted to the Native Americans through the 1868 Treaty of Fort Laramie. This was both a blessing and a curse for Deadwood, as the locals would soon find out.

I also dedicate this book to all the wonderful legendary characters of Deadwood, as well as the real-life proprietors, miners, gamblers, prostitutes, bartenders, outlaws, stagecoach drivers and everyone in between.

My hat goes off to these strong individuals who lived in an era when owning more than three outfits was considered a luxury, when one had to ride on the back of a horse and sleep under the stars for hundreds of miles, when people took the law into their own hands and hanged criminals from the nearest tree, when eking out a batch of dry biscuits from the few staples one had available just to feed the family was commonplace and when "dying with your boots on" was considered a privilege—although typically, the boots would be stolen from the corpse prior to burial. (*Hey, times were tough!*)

Note: All ages of the people in this book are approximate.

CONTENTS

ACKNOWLEDGMENTS

There are many people to thank for this endeavor, and without their help and guidance, this book would not have been possible. My always patient and wonderful senior acquisitions editor, Artie Crisp, and my ever-fabulous copyeditor, Zoe Ames, are always such a pleasure to work with, along with all the other incredible people at Arcadia Publishing and The History Press. Their enthusiasm for their mission to promote local history is infectious, and I am blessed to work on my books with them. Their dedication to recording local history is nothing less than amazing, and without them, many books would never be written.

A big thanks to all the people who work to promote Deadwood through their collections and attention to detail. Thank you to the hardworking folks at the Deadwood Historic Preservation archives; Deadwood History Inc.; the Historic Adams House & Museum; the Deadwood Public Library; the Black Hills Mining Museum; the Information Center; the Days of '76 Museum; Mount Moriah Cemetery; Deadwood Alive Shootouts and its reenactment of the Trial of Jack McCall; Homestake Adams Research and Cultural Center; and so many more! Without all your valuable time and energy, many historical artifacts, information and collections would be lost forever to the world.

And as always, I want to thank every single person who does what they can to preserve history—whether it is volunteering at the local historical society, maintaining old buildings that otherwise would get neglected or simply researching their private genealogy through sites like Ancestry.com. In this fast-paced and high-tech world, the past can, unfortunately, be forgotten, and every effort to maintain and record valuable data, photographs, diaries, documents and records is of the utmost importance for future generations.

> NOTE: Many of the stories in this book were pulled out of old newspapers, recapturing early Deadwood's fascinating history and unique characters. This book is not intended to be a definitive scholarly report, because even after hundreds of hours hunched over reading and researching articles, I still found conflicting dates, multiple variations of names and inconsistent historical details. I tried to be as accurate as possible, but don't forget that back then, people did not carry government-issued identification. Sometimes people would change their name on a whim, adopt a nickname or trade out their name for a different one to avoid the law. It was common for criminals to use multiple names—and just as many spellings.

Six unidentified men work to create and print a newspaper. Every single letter or number had to be placed manually in sequence (backward and in reverse order) for every page. *Courtesy of Library of Congress (hereafter LOC) #2004679585, Photo Department New York World, newspaper publishing, 1909.*

> Also remember that back in the old days, newspapers were printed using typesetters, and every single individual letter had to be set in place by hand and placed backward and in reverse order. These individual metal or wooden pieces were arranged inside a frame to form the content of each page of the newspaper, and each letter, punctuation mark and space was a separate physical piece. This process required considerable time, extreme patience, skill and precision. *Can you imagine?*

Some of the language or small details have been changed slightly or enhanced to benefit the story, but this is ultimately an account of the many lawless and wild people carousing around during the early days of Deadwood and the Black Hills. Tragically, these sinister, true tales all actually occurred.

So sit back with a glass of wine or a cup of coffee and transport yourself back in time—to a life before cell phones, automobiles, the internet, televisions and all the other modern luxuries we take for granted today.

I truly hope you enjoy reading *Deadwood Murder & Mayhem* as much as I enjoyed writing it!

INTRODUCTION

Deadwood, South Dakota, is located in the beautiful Black Hills region. Initially, the area was littered with lots of dead trees and dead stumps—thus the name Dead Wood. The town of Deadwood was formed inside a narrow gulch, surrounded by tall pines that consumed the daylight. In 1874–75, more trees fell down the steep grade, tumbling their way to the bottom of the gulch to lie and slowly rot. The area was so remote at the time that it was only accessible by horseback or bull train. But with hard work and determination, the dead trees were cleared out, and about forty rough cabins were built with any and all of the usable logs. By 1875, the town had grown to several thousand people and by June that year, supposedly thousands of grubstakes (supplies or money furnished to a mining prospector in exchange for the promise of a share in any gold, silver or ore one discovered). Soon, many men were in search of their fortune in gold among the Black Hills.

The historic Wild West town, nestled near Sturgis and Spearfish, now tantalizes over 2.5 million guests every year. So, whether you're intrigued to try your luck at gambling, interested in the town's rich history or simply enjoy fun outdoor adventures—*Deadwood is the place to be!*

Experience Deadwood through its historical reenactments, guided tours and a variety of other attractions and signature events. The Days of '76 Rodeo (one of the oldest rodeos in the whole country) still delights tourists. The Deadwood Jam Music Festival also draws a big crowd to the small town. There is always some sort of fun to be had in Deadwood.

Downtown Deadwood in 2024 as seen from Mount Moriah Cemetery, the final resting place for many local legends from the Old West, vicious murderers, wealthy madams and important men of early business development. *Courtesy of author.*

Today, just over one thousand people are lucky enough to call Deadwood their home. Many of the original buildings still stand, offering a fantastic look at some turn-of-the-century architecture. The location where Wild Bill Hickok was tragically shot in the back of the head is marked. The beautiful Mount Moriah Cemetery is worthy of a whole day's exploration. Please grab a copy of *Deadwood's Mount Moriah Cemetery* (Arcadia Publishing) by Michael W. Runge for a fascinating look into this massive graveyard and learn more about Deadwood's early pioneers.

Big-time Hollywood star Kevin Costner loved Deadwood. He became captivated by the Black Hills in 1990 while filming the movie *Dances with Wolves*, in which he plays the part of Lieutenant John Dunbar. Many scenes were shot in Spearfish Canyon and on the outskirts of Rapid City and Pierre. Costner purchased the Midnight Star Casino and Restaurant, but after twenty-six years of ownership, he decided to part ways with the Midnight Star. He also sold one thousand acres of land in the Black Hills in 2013.

NOTE: Visit the fascinating *Dances with Wolves* film set located at 2255 Fort Hayes Road, Rapid City, South Dakota, 57702, (888) 343-3113, for an inside look into the making of the movie. Also enjoy the Fort Hays Old West town and dinner show. The South Dakota Movie Museum showcases relics from over fifty other movies filmed in the state.

And of course, the famous HBO television series *Deadwood* (2004–06) ramped up everyone's interest in the small town.

The town's history is interwoven with unbelievable tales of mischievous cowboys and outlaws, eager gold prospectors and hardworking proprietors. Everyone knows about the local figures like Sol Star, Al Swearengen, Seth Bullock, Potato Creek Johnny and Calamity Jane who once roamed the streets of Deadwood, but there are countless other unknown pioneers who are just as fascinating.

It is always fun to discover details about the original pioneers and tidbits about Deadwood's early history. For instance, Pat Hulen and his party found the first bit of gold in Deadwood Gulch, and the Frank Bryant party also found gold, in August 1875, near Whitewood Creek in town. A man named Jack McAleer kept himself busy by building one of the first cabins. The town

Three old-timers (and their dog) seen panning for gold in South Dakota, hoping to strike it rich. The discovery of gold in the Black Hills near Deadwood in 1875–76 ignited a significant gold rush. *Courtesy of LOC #99613951, John C.H. Grabill, photographer, 1889.*

Left: The Midnight Star Casino was owned by famous actor Kevin Costner from 1991 until 2017. *Courtesy of author.*

Below: In the Deadwood Coach (the Cheyenne and Black Hills Stage), passengers were crammed together, and the route was prone to attacks by dangerous robbers. Its last trip was on December 28, 1890. *Courtesy of LOC #99613881, John C.H. Grabill, photographer, 1889.*

Opposite: Calamity Jane is buried next to legend Wild Bill Hickok in Mount Moriah Cemetery. She died in the Callaway Hotel in nearby Terry, virtually alone, from inflammation of the bowels. *Courtesy of author.*

was laid out on April 26, 1876, by Craver Lee, Isaac Brown and J.J. Williams—the busy Lee Street was named after Craver Lee. If one needed medical attention, they sought out the first *real* doctor in town, Dr. A.W. McKinney. The lawless town was always in need of good lawyers, and William George and Joseph Miller were kept very busy indeed. The first preacher in the Black Hills was Reverend Henry Smith (1828–1876, age forty-nine), who graced Deadwood in 1876. (Unfortunately, he was later murdered outside of Deadwood, and his assassin was never discovered.) As the town grew, so did its needs. So a man named George Stokes eagerly opened one of the first dry goods stores in the area, and the Big Horn Grocery was considered the first grocery store in Deadwood. One of the first attempts at a local theater was operated by Jack Langrishe; it opened in July 1876. Although it was nothing but a canvas roof with a dirt floor covered in sawdust, everyone seemed to enjoy it. The Northwestern Express stagecoach took three (or more!) days to get from Deadwood to Chicago and a very long and dusty thirty-three hours to travel from Deadwood to Pierre. In June 1876, the Boisset family opened the Bella Union Theater. One of their star entertainers was Mademoiselle Realta, renowned for her ability to somehow fire a five-hundred-pound cannon from her shoulder—*quite a sensation!*

In *Deadwood Murder & Mayhem*, we will step back in time and discover interesting true-life crimes committed in the Black Hills region when the days were long and the trails were dusty. I am hoping that as you read this book and visit Deadwood, the names will mean a little more to you and you will find the historic buildings a little more fascinating.

So sit back with your favorite beverage of choice and dive deep into these pages. I look forward to engaging you with these true-life accounts from the past. Perhaps I will entertain you just a bit—like Calamity Jane used to when she would gather a crowd around her, next to a crackling campfire, to listen to her tall (sometimes exaggerated) tales about the Wild West!

1
MURDERS IN DEADWOOD AND THE BLACK HILLS

"What is more important, that Caesar is assassinated or that he is assassinated by his intimate friends?... That," Frederick said, "is where the tragedy is."
—*M.L. Rio,* If We Were Villains

In the 1800s, the legal proceedings and punishments following misbehavior and murders varied greatly in severity and time served (if any). Sometimes, if a horrible man whom nobody liked was killed, the hastily organized group of miners and local men serving as makeshift "jurors" simply shrugged it off. The words "Who cares? He was a rat bastard and an asshole!" or "Nobody liked him anyway!" were muttered from many a pair of sun-chapped lips.

> NOTE: Download the panoramic photograph spanning the next two pages from the Library of Congress (item no. 2007662788), open it with Windows Photo Viewer (or a similar program) and you can zoom in on the picture and take a "virtual walk" through the streets of downtown Deadwood in 1909!

The brutal lynching of a man who committed murder was often a reckless and wild affair, with a posse of men jumping on their horses, hooting and hollering, rifles raised high above their heads as they spurred their horses onward. The killer, riding as fast as his horse could run, prayed the mob wouldn't catch up to him—but most of the time, the pursuers were successful.

A rope was tossed over the nearest, strongest tree and a hangman's noose formed on the other end. Sometimes the killer's hands were tied behind his back as he balanced precariously in his saddle, muttering, "Whoa" for his horse to stand still. The lawless lynchers were always nearby laughing, drinking and swearing at the doomed man, for they demanded justice.

Afterward, the deceased would hang there, dangling from the rope. Flies would swarm, the body would swell and a blue tongue would quickly protrude. Justice was served, all right.

During more respectable times, the killer(s) would be rounded up, dragged back and thrown into a jail cell to await the proper channels of justice.

There are several different types of murder, each having a different penalty.

MURDER: The gravest of crimes, where one human intentionally takes the life of another. In the old days, the noose awaited those who were found guilty. Murder comes in two forms:

FIRST DEGREE: The most serious form of homicide, an intentional and premeditated killing.

SECOND DEGREE: Less premeditated and typically occurring in the heat of the moment, often unplanned.

MANSLAUGHTER (sometimes called third-degree murder): A shade less sinister than murder. It encompasses two forms:

VOLUNTARY MANSLAUGHTER: The act of killing in the heat of passion or upon sudden provocation.

INVOLUNTARY MANSLAUGHTER: Unintentional killing due to reckless behavior or negligence.

Top: This panoramic photograph depicts Deadwood in 1909, population 3,498. In 1876, the population was at its peak: an estimated 12,000–25,000 people roamed the streets of Deadwood. *Courtesy of LOC #2007662788, F.J. Bandholtz, photographer, 1909.*

This page, bottom: In the early years, reckless lynchings of guilty parties were often executed by groups of vigilantes in the Black Hills, the corpses grisly reminders to others to obey the law. *Courtesy of LOC #2006687041, execution of Johnson, a colored soldier, for attempted rape, near Petersburg, Virginia, 1864.*

INFANTICIDE: A heart-wrenching crime—when a person takes the life of a newborn child.

FELONY MURDER: When someone dies during the commission of a felony (like robbery or arson), all involved may face murder charges.

ASSASSINATION: A targeted killing of a prominent figure—like a politician, monarch or rival.

SERIAL KILLING: The same hand orchestrating multiple deaths, often leaving investigators baffled.

POISONING: Subtle toxins slipped into cups, meals or medicines, sealing the fates of those targeted.

DUELS: Two men fighting to the death, pistols drawn in the street, with everyone watching.

CRIMES OF PASSION: Love, jealousy, rage—a volatile mix. When the heart breaks, murder often follows.

These definitions are especially important when it comes to understanding the sentences imposed on historical murderers. Locals often scratched their heads in disbelief when an admitted killer was acquitted and allowed to go free. The jury had their reasons, one supposes.

In 1878, Deadwood experienced eighteen murders in a brief time, with only one conviction. People began to gossip about the lawlessness of Deadwood, but Seth Bullock was always quick to point out that any persons calling Deadwood murderous were unworthy of the name of men and were vile slanderers. Yet that wasn't completely true. There was lots of violence and many out-of-control people in town.

In this chapter, we take a look at some of the more interesting murders in Deadwood's history. Within these pages, long-forgotten real-life characters are resurrected, and their crimes are retold. Baffling mysteries and unbelievable tales of woe are researched and addressed.

Sadly, many of these victims have simply been forgotten in time—lost somewhere on page 4 or 6 of the *Deadwood Daily Pioneer Times* or the *Black Hills Weekly Pioneer*, their deaths reduced to nothing more than a few sentences in faded ink. I am hoping to bring back to life these fallen heroes

Watch for these signs along the routes to Deadwood, marking various areas where the original wagon wheel ruts from stagecoaches still exist—a fascinating display from years gone by. *Courtesy of author.*

and notorious villains from Deadwood's fascinating past to explore and share with you.

Step back in time with me and try to visualize the bustling activities of the town, the sounds of gunfire and gambling and of horses' hooves and the creaking of wagon wheels. Try to imagine these deadly events as they played out and the unique characters who participated in them. These people actually once walked the streets of Deadwood and roamed the trails in the beautiful Black Hills. Hang on tight, for within these pages you are in for a bloody ride in a horsedrawn stagecoach on a dusty trail through Deadwood's fantastic history!

The First White Man Killed in the Black Hills

The first White man *reported* to have been killed in the Black Hills was a miner from Pioche, Nevada, named John (sometimes Jack) Hinch. He came to his death in Gayville in the early spring of 1876 at the hands of Jerry McCarty (also McCarthy) and John Carty.

Although the stories vary, the trouble commenced at a mining camp about two miles above Deadwood. On Sunday, July 10, 1876, John R. Carty, Jerry McCarty and a man named William Trainor (who later denied being there at the time of the incident) were gambling and drinking the night away at Billy Wilson's Saloon. About two o'clock in the morning, an onlooker, John Hinch, noticed that Carty and McCarty were getting desperate and beginning to cheat the other players out of their money.

Once the cheating was announced by Hinch and others, the poker game quickly came to a halt, and the cards were put away. The men would have to sort the problem out between themselves, Hinch thought. Tired, Hinch decided to head off to bed and get some much-needed rest. He made his way to the Turner & Wilson Saloon, where he was renting a room upstairs.

Disgruntled by Hinch's honesty, Carty and McCarty decided they wanted a fight, so they walked into the other saloon in search of Hinch. They made their way upstairs to his room and beat on the door.

"Get up and take a drink!" they ordered, but Hinch was in no mood. The men barged through his door at about the same time Hinch was getting up to tell them to go away.

Things quickly got out of hand. Carty hit Hinch over the head with his pistol, and then two shots were fired. McCarty viciously stabbed Hinch with a knife. Panicked, the two intruders ran from the bloody scene.

Poor Hinch lay there in agony until ten o'clock the next morning, when he finally died. Carty and McCarty, now sobering up and remembering what horrible deed they had done, quickly gave their mining claims to their landlord and a friend. Then they stole two horses and rode off to make their escape.

When the citizens of Gayville discovered the assault on Hinch, an angry three-man posse formed, for Hinch was well-liked in the small town. Authority to pursue and capture the murderers was hastily given to E.L. Edwards (a local blacksmith), Mr. Hinkel and Mr. Godfrey. The men would be given a hefty $1,000 for their valuable time and work in the matter.

Another $500 reward was also offered to locals for capturing the killers, which quickly escalated the search.

In the meantime, the assassins rode toward Fort Laramie, Wyoming, where the two decided it would be best to separate. McCarty would head toward Cheyenne, Wyoming, and Carty would jump aboard a train heading to Fort Fetterman, Wyoming.

The Gayville posse rode their horses all night and day until they arrived in Custer City, South Dakota (an incredible sixty-mile trek in the saddle). Edwards hopped aboard a train alone, hopefully heading in the same direction as the killers were, and the other two men headed back to Gayville. (It would have taken them four or more days to ride from Custer City to Fort Laramie on horseback.)

After a bit, U.S. Deputy Marshal Jack Davis captured Carty while on the train near Fort Laramie, Wyoming, and he was promptly arrested and hauled back to Deadwood Gulch to face trial.

A miners' jury (a makeshift group of locals) of seven men was set and ready to decide Carty's fate on July 31. It was noted that, the night of the murder, the killers asked the bartender at the Turner & Wilson Saloon, Mr. Wilson, to "turn the lights off" prior to the attack. This showed that the murder of Hinch was *premeditated*, which could drastically change the sentence imposed on the criminal.

But Carty gave a different version of the incident to the jurors:

> *About midnight my partner, Jerry McCarty, came into my room saying, "I have been robbed! I want my pistol and knife!" I said, "What in the devil is the matter with you, anyway? Get into bed and I will make it all right in the morning." He would not do as I told him and immediately started to the saloon of Mr. Wilson. After McCarty had been gone for about ten minutes, I got up and went to the saloon and found him there. I said to Mr. Wilson, "It's time to blow out the lights and close up, let's all take a drink then go home." This seemed to offend Mr. Hinch and he struck at me. I reacted to the blow by hitting him with the butt of my revolver. I hit him a second time and in doing so the revolver was discharged. I did not shoot at Hinch. I did not know that Hinch was stabbed until I was told so by McCarty. I said, "You damn son of a bitch! Get into the tent. You have got me into trouble." At this I immediately knocked McCarty down. I was sorry when I heard Hinch was hurt. I knew I had done wrong in hitting Hinch. I felt bad when I heard he was stabbed and sorry indeed when I learned he had a wife to mourn his loss. I told McCarty while on the road to throw away the knife—told him I did not wish to see it again. These are the facts and I tell them as such, though I may die in a minute's time. That is all.*[1]

After the jury deliberated for one and a half hours, the verdict was read: "We find the prisoner guilty of assault and battery."

Another version of the story later surfaced. Rumors spread that Hinch had found gold in Gayville and had his eye on it. He decided to meet up with McCarty and Carty and start some trouble. The three men exchanged words in a saloon, and McCarty pulled a knife, stabbing Hinch. The men fled the scene. Carty later returned to Gayville to confess his misdoings in the matter. A makeshift trial was held in the local bakery, and the jury found Carty not guilty.

Jerry McCarty was later captured while on a train headed for San Francisco, California. He was indicted for the murder of Hinch but, of course, pled not guilty, on October 13, 1876. He went to jail for the murder, but oddly, in 1877, he was discharged after the prosecution entered a nolle prosequi (pronounced "NAH-lee PRAH-suh-kwi," this means "unwilling to pursue." It is used when a prosecutor decides to voluntarily drop or dismiss charges against a defendant for lack of evidence, lack of witnesses or as part of a plea bargain), dismissing the charges. McCarty eagerly promised that intoxicating liquors would never again touch his lips. Officials and locals agreed that McCarty had spent enough time in prison and that his stay behind bars had given him a new perspective on life and the grave results of his alcohol overconsumption.

Hinch was buried at Whitewood Gulch. The illegal transfers of McCarty and Carty's mining claims in Gayville were to be given to his widow as compensation for his untimely death.

The seven jurors decided that Hinch's death was the result of his wounds and that the killing was without just cause or provocation, but the killers still barely got a slap on the wrist. In this case, many people felt justice was not served.

Ghastly Triple Murder at Sawpit Gulch

Just two miles from Deadwood, between Blacktail Gulch and Bobtail Gulch, was a small grouping of homes in what was then called Sawpit Gulch, located near Central City. On a gloomy day in 1893, a horrific triple murder and suicide in Sawpit Gulch rocked the whole community. The killer, Joseph Giuseppe Tha, was originally from Italy, and it was known that he had a violent temper. The warning signs were there, but unfortunately, they were either ignored or went unnoticed.

Even worse (if there is anything worse), the bloody crimes were committed right in front of the family's two-and-a-half-year-old son and a twenty-month-old baby.

What started out as an innocent commitment to bring Ms. Quintina Bontempo over from Italy and the resulting marriage to Tha on June 3 quickly escalated into a gruesome nightmare. Not too long after Quintina arrived, Tha began abusing her. She refused to allow him to continually beat her, so she moved into the home of her aunt, Mrs. Jacco Tammitta (also Tamietti). Quintina told her aunt and uncle that she was afraid of Tha and she wished for an immediate divorce. She even went into Deadwood to file a formal complaint against Tha for spousal abuse. Sheriff Remer quickly placed Tha under bonds and sternly told the other man to keep the peace. But that did little to deter Tha. He had threatened to kill everyone if Quintina refused to move back home with him. He even went so far as to put explosives in Mr. and Mrs. Tammitta's woodshed as a scare tactic. Tha was arrested again but quickly released.

SHERIFF, ASSISTANTS AND DESPERATE INDIAN OUTLAWS

The Deadwood jail is now housing a group of criminals the like of which has probably never been gathered under a single roof. Lined up above are 1. Three Bears, murder; 2. Charging Cat, murder; 3. Alexandria Bertrand, jailer; 4. Switchtails of Amos, murder; 5. William A. Remer, sheriff; 6. Two Arrows, rape; 7. James D. Harding, deputy sheriff; 8. Eagle Louse, murder; 9. Alvin M. Clark, deputy sheriff; 10. Red Elk, murder; 11. Kills The Two, murder.

Front left to right: Alex Bertrand (jailor), Sheriff William Remer, Deputy Sheriff James Harding and Deputy Sheriff Alvin Clark. The silhouettes of criminals are in the background. *Courtesy of the* Black Hills Weekly Pioneer, *June 8, 1876.*

At noon that fateful day, Tha left the Golden Reward Boarding House at Bald Mountain, where he was living, and went to work at Tony Bareleno's (also sometimes spelled Bertolino's) mine. He decided to quit work early, at ten thirty that morning, because he had already secretly made plans to conduct the killings.

"When will you return?" his boss, Tony, asked him.

"If I don't return by this evening, I will never return," Tha said calmly.[2] Then he made his way to an area where he practiced firing his pistol. He then returned to the Golden Reward Boarding House and had a bite to eat, but he was already so drunk and obnoxious that his landlady, Mrs. O'Leary, was afraid of him.

While intoxicated, Tha drove to Sawpit Gulch and banged on the front door of the Tammitta home. Mrs. Tammitta opened the door slowly and firmly demanded that Tha leave the premises. Angry, Tha pushed past her and illegally entered the residence. Nearby neighbors heard violent noises and screams coming from the house but neglected to call the police.

Around two o'clock that afternoon, a vegetable peddler knocked on the front door of the Tammittas' house, as he often sold his fresh produce to the family. When no one answered the door, he knocked again. Then he heard loud cries coming from the children. Startled, he knocked once more, but there was again no answer. Concerned, he slowly opened the door, calling out, "Mrs. Tammitta? Are you there?"

What he saw inside the house would haunt him forever. A blood-soaked Tha lay on the floor, surrounded by a pool of his own blood. A bullet from a .38 caliber weapon had passed through his brain. His Smith & Wesson revolver was still in his blood-covered hand. A bloody axe lay nearby.

Somehow, Tha was still alive.

The peddler fled the scene to notify the police. Deputy Sheriff Brad Wood was called to the scene. Coroner Stein and Dr. Dickinson were right behind him.

The Scene

The small kitchen in the Tammittas' house was around eight feet by ten feet. The family had obviously been in the middle of lunch when Tha attacked them. Mr. Jacco Tammitta had been shot in the chest, neck and right arm. His wife, once a beautiful and robust woman, lay nearby with her head crushed by the axe. She had also been shot two times in her right leg. Young

Quintina was lying between the stove and the table, face down in a pool of her own blood. Tha had shot her directly in her mouth. In total, eight shots had been fired—he saved the ninth bullet for himself.

The brutal killer, Tha, was found in the sitting room area, gun still in his hand, moaning in pain. He had shot himself in the neck (the bullet's pressure popping out his left eye, as he was right-handed), and the bullet traveled upward and was now lodged somewhere inside his brain.

The Investigation

It was discovered that Tha had showed up very drunk at the Tammittas' house around noon. He immediately went after his wife and shot her in the face as she screamed. Mr. Tammitta quickly grabbed an axe and rushed toward Tha in self-defense. Tha pulled the axe away from him and hit Mrs. Tammitta over the head with it a few times; then he shot Mr. Tammitta without a moment's hesitation.

Tha, now exhausted from his ravenous murder frenzy, moved to the sitting room, pointed the gun at himself and pulled the trigger.

The Bodies

Tha was dead by five thirty the afternoon of the murders.

The bodies of the victims were taken to Burr Beckwith's house.

Quintina is buried at St. Ambrose Cemetery in Deadwood. Tha is buried in the South Potters Field.

This is an example of a horrific tragedy that could have been avoided if early warning signs were not ignored. Quintina, a woman who simply wanted to make a new life for herself in America, was now dead. The family members who were innocently trying to protect her from her abusive husband were also now all dead.

May their souls rest in peace.

MURDER AT QUEEN OF THE HILLS

In 1905, the murder of a handsome young man named Michael Richard Galvin (1877–1905, age twenty-seven) sparked a debate in Deadwood.* The murderer, local Eli Porter Farnham (1868–1922, age fifty-three), was a known loose cannon suffering from various mental complications.

Mining for gold was becoming increasingly popular in the Black Hills, and everyone wanted a piece of the profits. Farnham, a working man, was no different.

Earlier, in 1900, Farnham was appointed postmaster of Central City, where he also had a small store and a private home. His troubles started in February 1905, when he decided it would be a good idea to burn down the buildings to collect the insurance money. Several witnesses put him at the arson scene the day of the fire—which resulted in a complete loss of the structures. G.M. Martin, a carpenter in Central City, watched Farnham enter the front of the post office building (which normally wouldn't be unusual, since he was the postmaster) carrying some sort of can. Others indicated that Farnham reeked of kerosene and coal oil; both his trousers and shoes smelled heavily of it. The manager at the Shannon Hotel told officials that she'd noticed Farnham was day drinking prior to the fire. Locals had noticed Farnham's increased interest in getting really drunk. A bartender said that on the day of the fire, Farnham purchased two bottles of brandy from the Birch Saloon, located across the street from the Shannon House Hotel. These and more subtle clues alerted the police and insurance claims adjusters that there was more to the story than just an accidental fire.

During their investigation, Farnham was away in Nebraska for business, but authorities were waiting patiently for him to disembark the train in Deadwood on his return.

On February 17, Farnham was arrested for arson. He stated he was not feeling very well and begged the arresting officer to allow him to stay the night at the Franklin Hotel instead of going to the slammer. It was agreed that he could spend the night at the Franklin Hotel and be brought to the courthouse first thing in the morning, but he would have to be guarded by an on-duty night watchman so he could not escape. Farnham agreed.

The next day, Farnham was indicted by a grand jury for arson. His bail was quickly paid, and he walked away from behind bars. (He had withdrawn

* Most newspaper articles spell it "Gavin," but his tombstone spells it "Galvin."

Days before Eli Farnham brutally killed Michael Galvin, he collected Galvin's mail from the post office and noticed a handwritten letter from his wife to Galvin, fueling his insane jealousy. *Courtesy of the* Black Hills News-Letter and Mining Reporter, *December 30, 1878.*

After his arrest for arson, Eli Farnham was allowed to stay the night in comfort at the Franklin Hotel (pictured) instead of at the jail until his trial. *Courtesy of author.*

Eli Farnham was found mentally unstable, so he was quickly checked out from the Franklin Hotel (pictured), his belongings were packed up and he was sent off to a mental hospital for recovery. *Courtesy of author.*

$2,862 and $4,754 from Black Hills Savings & Trust a week earlier, probably knowing he would need money for his release or possibly intending to secure getaway funds.) He also resigned as postmaster.

Farnham's lawyer claimed he was not mentally stable, so after his sentencing, his belongings were packed up from his room at the Franklin Hotel and he was sent to a mental hospital for recovery. He slowly healed his mind and was released to secure work.

After his discharge from the psych ward, Farnham found employment as the superintendent of the Queen of the Hills Gold Mining Company near Whistler Gulch, about one and a half miles outside of Deadwood. The young Michael Galvin had also worked at the Queen, as the foreman, going on now for over a year.

Eli Farnham's wife, Nora Skelton Farnham (1868–1929, age sixty-one), was excellent with the books and daily dealings of the family, so she worked hard keeping all the money straight. Farnham often had fits of jealousy and accused Galvin and Nora of improper relations, but there was no valid reason for his bitterness. A few days before the shooting, Farnham went to the Deadwood Post Office to fetch the mail. He also requested to pick up Galvin's mail to "save the young man a trip into town." But red flags waved in front of his eyes again as he noticed his own wife's handwriting on one of the envelopes addressed to Galvin. Visions of his wife and Galvin together in bed raced through his thoughts, infuriating him. He tore open the letter, expecting sweet words about a romantic tryst or a lovers' secret meeting. Instead, it was a letter explaining away a business deal Mr. Farnham was working on, which would leave Mr. Farnham $3,000, Nora $1,000 and Galvin $500.

Suddenly, Farnham didn't know which annoyed him more, that Galvin was involved in his business or possibly screwing around with his wife. He probably muttered, "I'm gonna kill that son of a bitch!" under his breath as he left the post office.

Just the year before, Farnham had actively accused Galvin of having sex with his wife, at which Galvin protested profusely. When approached by locals about the supposed infidelity, Galvin yelled,

> *As far as I am concerned personally, it does not matter what Mr. Farnham or anyone else may say, but I do not want to see an innocent woman suffer and I do not want my own father and brothers to believe I have been guilty of such immoral conduct as Farnham refers to. My associations with Mrs. Farnham have always been of the most proper and I believe she is faithful and attached to her husband.*[3]

Yet Nora's love for her husband may have been waning, as he was reportedly abusive toward her. He flew off into unwarranted jealous tirades and once even locked her out of the house and then proceeded to get stinking drunk.

Galvin was growing tired of Farnham's accusations and decided it would be best to quit the Queen and gain employment at the Homestake Mine in Lead. He sold his Queen claims for $200 to John Vigna, a man who lived on a small cabin on the mine's property.

Around noon on March 13, everything came to a boiling point. Farnham and a few others were in the dining room in the bunkhouse of the Queen having lunch together. The men noticed Galvin riding up the trail on his horse toward the bunkhouse.

Farnham's face turned as white as a ghost. He quickly left the building, leaving brothers Alonzo and Winzor Torrence wondering what was going

Unidentified miners inside Homestake with large timber supports. Work conditions were brutal, and over four hundred men were killed in the mine. Its deepest point was eight thousand feet (one and a half miles) below the surface! *Courtesy of LOC #2012648316, William Perkins Jr., photographer, 1908.*

to happen next. Nobody knew it at the time, but Galvin was simply there to collect his last paycheck before going to work for the Homestake Mine.

Soon Farnham returned, his face now red and not white—and he was eagerly holding a shotgun he stole from Vigna's cabin. The two enemies met in front of the bunkhouse. "Why don't you stay off this ground?! Isn't it enough for you that you have broken up my family? Now go on down the gulch and quit following me! You black-legged son of a bitch!"

"I will go over this ground anywhere I please!" Galvin yelled back.[4] The men proceeded to scuffle and punch each other.

Suddenly, a thunderous shot was fired. Farnham quickly dropped the weapon. In an instant, Galvin had his hands around Farnham's throat, trying to strangle the man.

The Torrence brothers ran to try to break up the fight. Winzor grabbed the shotgun from the ground and busted Galvin over his head with it, which seemed to do the trick.

But everyone froze as they watched Galvin stand up, bright red blood oozing from his right side and soaking through his shirt. The Torrence boys quickly loaded Galvin up in Farnham's one-horse buggy and drove as quickly as the horse could gallop to St. Joseph's Hospital in Deadwood.

At the hospital, the Sisters tended to Galvin's wounds, packing and dressing them, hoping to slow down the bleeding. When Dr. Babcock examined Galvin, he was hopeful—but not very. Galvin had suffered a bullet through his right side that fractured four ribs and damaged his internal organs, all resulting in massive blood loss. His worried brother Seth stayed by his side, praying Galvin would pull through.

Sheriff Martin Ellingston rode out to Queen of the Hill and promptly arrested Farnham, who did not put up much of a fight. Farnham just shrugged, because in his mind, he had acted in self-defense, believing Galvin was actually there to kill him.

Meanwhile, Galvin was the one fighting for his life in St. Joseph's Hospital. He was in complete agony. Sadly, the doctors felt there was nothing more they could do for him. Galvin, knowing death was near, wished for his dying declaration to be written up. His brother Seth and one of the Sisters listened to his story and slowly wrote it down for him. In a nutshell, Galvin recounted how he was taking a shortcut through the Queen property to his own property when Farnham confronted him and threatened to kill him. Galvin rushed at him after the first shot was fired, hoping to secure the shotgun from his enemy before a second fatal shot could be fired.

After Galvin's deathbed report was given to the police, Farnham was quickly placed behind bars with a $10,000 bail bond hanging over his head.

Michael Richard Galvin took his last breath at 3:10 p.m. on March 18, just five days after he was tragically shot. The coroner later discovered that he had also suffered from blood poisoning due to his wounds.

Galvin was born in Missouri and moved to the Black Hills with his family in 1881. He was considered a complete gentleman of good character by everyone who knew him.

After a ten-day trial, the twelve-man jury spent three hours deliberating over the case. Farnham was acquitted of Galvin's murder (possibly due to his mental health issues), but he was tried a second time for arson and insurance fraud. (Some records indicate he was found not guilty of those, too.)

Nora later divorced Eli Farnham and made a home for herself in Yankton, South Dakota, where she lived until her death in 1929. She is buried at the State Hospital Cemetery.

Farnham remarried in 1908 and moved to Las Animas, Colorado, where he lived until his death in 1922.

Gunshot victim Galvin never got the chance to be married, never had a family and never got to live his life to its fullest potential. The unwarranted jealousy of a man with an unstable mind took those chances away from him in a quick flash with the help of a stolen gun.

Justice was not properly served in this case, no doubt. Galvin's family was left with only heartache and loss. Michael was lovingly buried next to his mother, Mary Galvin (1847–1884, age thirty-six), in the family plot in Galena, South Dakota.

AN EXPLODING TIRE PUMP AND DEATH

The murder of a well-liked man named Frank Sterling Peck (1861–1926, age sixty-four) shocked the small community of Deadwood. Born in Nodaway, Missouri, Peck came to the Black Hills at age nineteen, rolling into town in 1880. Peck eventually became a civil engineer for the local highway department. He lived peacefully with his wife, Martha Baxter (1870–1959, age eighty-nine; listed as Matilda in the 1920 census), and son Francis (1898–1962, age sixty-four). Peck was an active member of the Deadwood Fire Department and the Deadwood Lodge No. 7. But in the early morning hours of September 6, 1926, the Peck family was thrown into massive turmoil that would end in tragedy.

The night before, Peck had noticed an old tire pump lying on the side of the street near where he kept his Studebaker automobile on Charles Street. Not thinking much of it, he passed it off as garbage. But at seven o'clock that following morning, he got curious about whether the pump worked or not, so he casually picked it up. When he went to try the pump, a terrible explosion instantly occurred—shattering both his legs from the knees down and paralyzing his stomach. For some reason, the tire pump had been filled with nitroglycerine. Nitroglycerin is a very dangerous, oily liquid that explodes when subjected to heat, shock or flame.

Peck lay in horrible agony until James Peirce ran to his aid. Acting as local coroner and doctor, Mr. Dodges was called in, and Peck was whisked off to St. Joseph's Hospital. The doctors amputated his right foot and then

An unidentified group of Deadwood engineers with surveying equipment in 1888. One of the men could possibly be Frank Peck, who was savagely murdered in 1926 in Deadwood. *Courtesy of LOC #99613819 and #99613820, John C.H. Grabill, photographer, Deadwood Central R.R. Engineer Corps.*

his left leg below the knee. Peck suffered for another three exceptionally long, painful days, and his condition worsened. It was a horrible and sad tragedy. His family stayed at his bedside, praying and hoping Peck would pull through the surgeries. But their prayers went unanswered.

Peck died from his wounds at 10:40 a.m. on September 10, after four days of complete agony. His funeral was held at the Masonic Temple in Deadwood, and the building was filled to capacity with the people who loved and respected him. The whole town was in mourning. Flags were hung at half-mast. Peck was a devoted father, a loving husband and a good citizen of Deadwood. Locals had watched Peck grow from a teenage boy to a hardworking man in their town.

Surely, a full investigation would find and punish his ruthless killer! Police followed every possible lead in the puzzling case. After a consuming amount of time and energy, Rudolf Fredericks, a thirty-eight-year-old Boulder Canyon rancher, was charged with Peck's murder. Rumors had been spreading that Fredericks was angry at Peck about an accident that occurred: William "Bert" Fredericks, Rudolf's brother, had been killed while also working for the city. Peck was the supervisor in charge of the work crew when William was killed—and Rudolf was still harboring a grudge.

Although the family received an insurance payout for William's demise, Rudolf was irritated that the settlement offered only payments in installments; he desired one lump sum.

After nine months in the Lawrence County Jail, Rudolf was released due to insufficient evidence that he was the killer.

Then another man, Jack Gray, confessed to the Peck incident to his recent ex-wife, who was living in Deadwood. After being followed through Montana, North Dakota and Wisconsin, he was finally arrested in Crandon, Wisconsin, in 1928 and charged in connection with Peck's murder. Gray would be held in Crandon until Deadwood authorities could arrive for him.

A Deadwood detective arrived and questioned Gray, who told authorities he denied all involvement in Peck's death, although he was guilty of stealing some alfalfa seed. Perhaps Gray's ex-wife was just trying to stir up trouble for him?

Peck's murder was never solved. There were never any more leads or convictions in the matter. To this day, the truth behind the tragedy that killed Peck remains another Deadwood mystery. May his kind soul rest in peace.

THE MASCOT SALOON AND A LOVERS' TRIANGLE

The winters in the Black Hills can be long and brutal. Everyone's nerves are on edge, and the drinking can get mighty heavy. For a couple of Deadwood locals, the night of December 17, 1893, would end a bloody one.

The Mascot Saloon was a favorite watering hole in town, and the saloon portion was divided by two separate wine rooms. There was Wine Room No. 1 at the rear of the bar and Wine Room No. 2 more toward the front.

On December 17, Mary Yousta (also Yusta) was drinking with Frank DeBelloy down at the Mascot. They thought it would be funny to have Maggie McDermott come down to join them for a drink. Mary wrote a note inviting her and handed it to the bartender, M.J. Donovan. "Run this note over to Maggie, will you? She is in room No. 3 at the Gib Stone Building," Mary said.[5] Donovan was busy tending bar, so he handed the note to Nick Sargen, requesting he do the errand instead.

Maggie got the note, which simply said, **Come down to the Mascot, Frank and I are here.** Maggie, with her friend Hattie Rice, decided to go to the Mascot to address Mary's invitation. She did not think the private joke was very funny.

Maggie's blood was already boiling as the girls stormed into Wine Room No. 2, where Mary was sitting. Mary raised her drink to Maggie. "Maggie, I sent for you to have a drink with us," she said.[6]

"I don't like your nerve to be here with Frank when I have more claim on him than you, we having been together for the past three years,"[7] Maggie yelled, tearing up the note and throwing it in Mary's face. "You goddamn whore! I would not drink with a goddamn whore like you!"[8]

Hattie became very uncomfortable. She wanted to leave the bar. "Come on, Maggie, let's go," she cried.

"If I can't have him, you can't either!"[9] Mary cried as she moved away and quickly pulled something from her purse. Suddenly, two shots were fired. A thick red stain began spreading across Maggie's chest. Frank grabbed the gun from Mary's hand, and the two started to argue.

Maggie slowly made her way out of Wine Room No. 2 and headed toward Wine Room No. 1. "She shot me," she told Donovan behind the bar. Frantic, Frank gave the weapon to the bartender for safekeeping. "Shit!" said Donovan as he ran to get a doctor. Maggie lay down on a nearby sofa to rest. "Mary Yousta shot me," she whispered.[10]

One bullet had moved through Maggie's right breast, hitting her sixth rib, liver, lung and spleen.

Chief of Police Diltz quickly came to the scene, and Donovan handed him the murder weapon.

Poor Maggie died within five minutes, for there was no way to save her.

Frank and Mary were arrested and charged with Maggie's murder. There were plenty of witnesses, so the trial should have been an easy one—but there's always more to the story.

It came to light that Frank had given Mary the gun just the day before—so that she could kill Maggie! Mary lived at the Castle (also called the 400 House); that's where Frank gave her the weapon.

The trial dragged on, and in the spring of 1894, sentences were announced. Sixteen-year-old Mary (originally from Austria) was found guilty of manslaughter in the second degree. The judge could have confined her to prison for a maximum of four years behind bars. But because of her young age, she was granted some leeway and ended up in a youth reform school instead. Frank was acquitted, as the jury decided he was present but not involved in the actual shooting of Maggie.

This cold-blooded Deadwood murder presents some gray areas. Many locals were left scratching their heads as questions arose about the tragic incident. If Frank gave Mary the gun to kill Maggie, why did the jury not take that into consideration? Wasn't he an accomplice? Sixteen seems young to be drinking in a bar (but then again, it *was* 1893, and it *was* Deadwood). Mary's very weak self-defense was, "I thought Maggie was going to kill me with a chair." Yet Maggie was over three feet away from Mary when she raised the chair. But in Mary's defense, many residents of the 400 House came forward to state that Maggie had threatened to kill a few people in town, which would have caused Mary to be in a state of fear.

Henry Clark: Killed Over a Saddle?

Henry Clay Clark (1837–1883, age forty-five or forty-six) was reportedly born in Norfolk, Virginia (as listed on his military transcripts from 1864). Other conflicting records indicate he was born on a ship off Cape Hatteras that tragically sank shortly after his birth. (Supposedly, no ship records listed at the Mystic Sea Museum in Connecticut can confirm this information either.) Sadly, legend says that his father, Captain Clark, went down with his ship and that Henry's mother was rescued along with her babe.

As an adult, Clark worked as an auctioneer and also became a deacon. He lived in Denver, Colorado, on Blake Street. Later in life, he owned some interests in the California Gulch in Leadville, Colorado, and was part owner of the Elephant Corral in Denver County.

Clark came rolling into Deadwood in July 1876 or '77 and became one of the original pioneers of the town. He married Mary Lenore Steinagle (1832–1866, age thirty-four), who died just two years after the birth of their daughter, Lillian (1864–1944, age eighty). He later remarried Kate Horst (1837–1916, age seventy-eight).

Clark owned a store called Edmond's Auction House. A cranky carpenter named Thomas B. Rollins worked for him, and they often quarreled. Rollins lived in Deadwood at 453 Gold Street. In the winter of 1883, the arguing finally came to a boiling point. Rollins had borrowed a saddle from the store without Clark's permission, and to make matters worse, he sold the saddle and kept the money for himself! The men began fighting yet again, and Rollins suddenly grabbed a nearby axe. He swung the weapon at Clark, knocking him down, and then proceeded to hit him with a hammer. Clark suffered from a broken jaw and a massive poke injury from an instrument in his right eye and had four teeth knocked from his mouth.

Rollins was arrested, taken to the Justice Hall and then thrown in jail. The Honorable Judge William Church set bail at $2,000. Rollins, of course, pled not guilty.

A hearing was held, and Rollins was tried and acquitted for the murder of Henry Clark. The reasons for this are unclear, but it was probably due to the claims of self-defense presented by his lawyer during the trial. Rollins claimed that Clark had initiated a violent altercation, and witnesses corroborated that Clark had acted aggressively and posed an imminent threat to Rollins.

Clark died later on the same day as the confrontation that occurred with Rollins on February 13, 1883. His body was taken to Smith's Undertaking, and Drs. O'Neall and Dickinson were his coroners. He is buried in Mount Moriah Cemetery in Deadwood. Later, in October the same year, E. Carl purchased his old store on lower Main Street in Deadwood.

The brutal murder of Henry Clark remains another early Deadwood tragedy.

Al Swearengen's Mysterious Death

Deadwood. A hell of a place to make a living.
—Al Swearengen, proprietor, Gem Variety Theatre

A book about murder and mayhem in Deadwood would not be complete without a chapter on one of the most notorious bad guys in town, Al Swearengen (1845–1904, age fifty-nine). His name is also often spelled Swearingin; his full name was Ellis Alfred or Ellis Albert or simply E.A.

Swearengen was born on July 8, 1845, in Oskaloosa, Iowa Territory. His parents were Daniel J. Swearengen and Keziah "Katie" Montgomery. His twin brother, Lemuel Abraham Swearengen (1845–1910, age sixty-five), would later play a role in his untimely demise.

Swearengen arrived in Deadwood sometime in May 1876, with his young wife, Nettie Clifford (1852–1884?, age thirty-two).* Unfortunately, their marriage ended in divorce due to spousal abuse. (He married twice more, and both of these marriages also ended in divorce due to physical abuse.)

In Deadwood, Swearengen initially owned and operated a canvas-roof saloon called the Cricket, where he held prize fights that drew big crowds. (The location of the old Cricket Saloon is now where the small Lucky Horse Company souvenir shop is located, at 621 Main Street, nestled between the new Gem Steakhouse & Saloon/Mineral Palace located at 601 Main Street and the Celebrity Hotel at 629 Main. Sales from the Lucky Horse store help fund the rescue and care of local animals in need.)

After some financial success, Swearengen opened the Gem Variety Theatre on April 7, 1877, at the corner of Wall and Main Streets in Deadwood. Although his personal attributes were highly questionable, he was a magnificent proprietor when it came to entertaining people and making money. He brought in big new talent to the Gem—along with young women who were forced into becoming soiled doves. Swearengen was well known for luring pretty, innocent girls to Deadwood, pretending they would have secure office work when they arrived. But then Al would put them up in his hotel, and without any means of income, they would soon have to slip into the underworld of working as a prostitute to support themselves and pay their rent.

---

* Some records indicate that Nettie died from a combination of whiskey and morphine in 1884. Whether her death was an accident or suicide is unknown. Other records indicate she lived to the ripe old age of ninety-four and died in 1946.

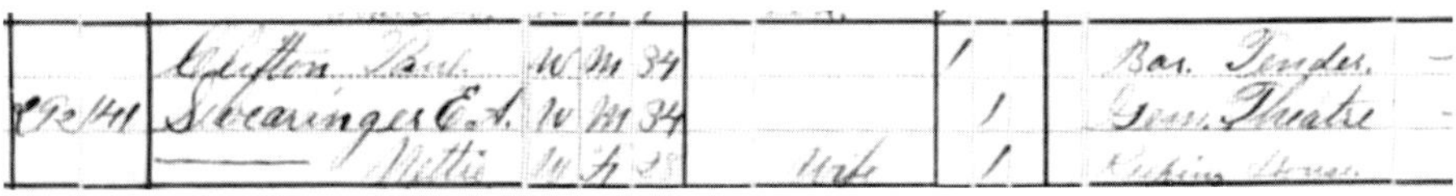

		Clifton Paul	W	M	34		1	Bar Tender
292	141	Swearenger E.A.	W	M	34		1	Gem Theatre
		—— Nettie	W	F	28	Wife	1	Keeping House

Records from the 1880 Deadwood census showing E.A. (Al) Swearengen (of the Gem Theatre, age thirty-four) and Nettie ("keeping house," age twenty-eight) and Paul Clifton (bartender, age thirty-four) all living at 292 Main Street. *Courtesy of Ancestry.com.*

But Swearengen was not the only one profiting from sex workers. Local madams like Dirty Em and Madame Mustachio were pocketing 40 percent of their working girls' profits. (A top-earner prostitute would receive twenty dollars in gold dust for sleeping with a man.)

The Gem quickly became the chief attraction in Deadwood, serving as a full saloon; a gambling hall; an active dance spot, with live music nightly; and a very busy brothel. One of the more popular acts was a team called Smith and Bennington, who could play fourteen different musical instruments. Another fun act at the Gem was sketch artists Martin and Murdy. The Petronelli Sisters also kept the place shaking. Ads were run for the Gem in the local newspapers, touting "ballad singing, banjo playing, bone-rattling, tambo whacking, comic acts, sketches, and droll doings."

Unfortunately, the original Gem suffered from a fire on September 26, 1879. Swearengen quickly rebuilt the place even bigger and better than it was before, reopening it in December 1879.

In 1880, a new star at the Gem was picking up speed. Fannie Douglass was considered the best comic vocalist ever to exist. A troupe from New York graced the stage in 1882 when the town's population was still fairly large: sixteen thousand. And the prize fights continued no matter what. The citizens loved to see blood and bet on their favorite men.

Swearengen was street-smart, and he frequently rubbed shoulders with very prominent authorities, thus granting him immunity from most legal repercussions. Even the upright and incorruptible Marshal Seth Bullock quietly backed off on his efforts to clean up the lower regions of Main Street, where the Gem operated nightly.

But Swearengen's immunity didn't always get him off the hook. In 1881, he was fined one hundred dollars for selling liquor without a license.

In 1884, the Gem was busier than ever. Swearengen began promoting grand dress balls and advertising events that would "take the cake," at which the bar would be stocked with "the finest liquors and best cigars in the entire Black Hills!" He also advertised that the girls would be "attentive and witty."

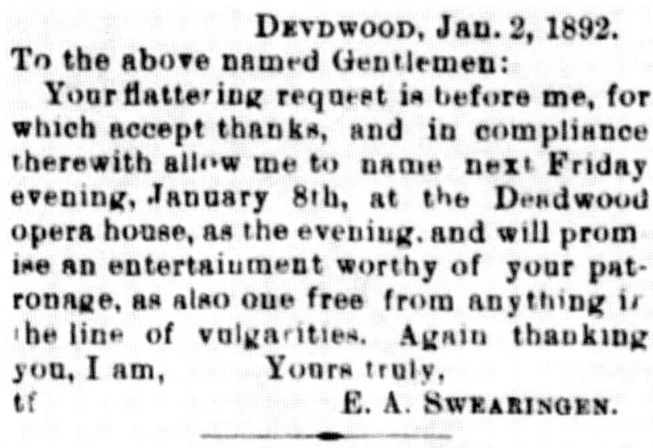

Devdwood, Jan. 2, 1892.
To the above named Gentlemen:
Your flattering request is before me, for which accept thanks, and in compliance therewith allow me to name next Friday evening, January 8th, at the Deadwood opera house, as the evening, and will promise an entertainment worthy of your patronage, as also one free from anything in the line of vulgarities. Again thanking you, I am, Yours truly,
tf E. A. Swearingen.

Al Swearengen placed ongoing ads in the local newspaper offering apologies and extending an invitation to his opera house on January 2, promising a night without vulgarities. *Courtesy of the* Black Hills Daily Times, *January 5, 1892.*

The Gem's nightly earnings were staggering, averaging around $5,000 and sometimes reaching as high as $10,000.*

In 1887, Al was charged with keeping a disorderly house. In 1891, he was arrested again, this time by Officer Conners, but he quickly posted bail just in time to play his role in the production of *Jack the Ripper* on his stage at the Gem.

In 1892, the Gem was still hopping. Poker and faro games were raging, although the stakes had dropped down to around $3,000 per night. Someone thought it would be funny to post a Pastor's Study sign over the entrance to the poker room, and supposedly, the players would start each card game with an opening prayer.

In 1893, Swearengen appeared before the judge again for malicious mischief; he pled guilty and was fined ten dollars. That same year, he got in trouble for thumping one of the local working girls, Hattie Lewis, on her head with an Indian club. He had accused her of stealing $1,000 in large bills from the Gem, which she denied. (Suspiciously, her piano player friend left town to break the large bills elsewhere.)

Rumors that Swearengen had a hog barn outside of Deadwood where one could secretly and discreetly dispose of a dead body were floating around, but perhaps that was just a scare tactic from Al. There was, however, a documented "meat-packaging plant" just behind the Gem building, so one never knows.

On July 3, 1889, Al married Odelia Turgeon in Deadwood.

* $5,000 in 1904 is equivalent in purchasing power to about $175,467 today.

Scantily clad dancers like this one graced the stage at the Gem Variety Theatre, delighting and arousing men, which promoted the sexual services of Swearengen's ladies offered upstairs. *Courtesy of LOC#2018707214, dancer Genthe Arnold, by Hilda Beyer, photographer, 1913.*

Also in 1899, a second fire burned the Gem to the ground. After running a profitable saloon in Deadwood for twenty-two years, Al had had enough of fires and rebuilding and decided to leave town for good. His whereabouts over the next few years remain sketchy. But in mid-October 1903, he returned to Deadwood on a Burlington train from the West after a long absence, announcing he was back in Deadwood for good and wanted to remain there. He said he had been living in Dawson in the Northwest Territory (it's unclear in which state) for the past couple of years. His old pals and enemies all remarked that Al had never looked happier or healthier, and Swearengen himself bragged about the fact that he had never felt better in his life.

So what happened to Al in the months that followed? What prompted his change of heart, from wanting to stay in Deadwood and leaving it? Did he receive threats? Was he holding a dark secret? Why did he suddenly flee his beloved hometown of Deadwood?

Sometime between October 1903 and November 1904, Al Swearengen, the infamous saloon owner from Deadwood, lived for a brief period in his hometown of Oskaloosa, Iowa. At some point, he moved away and began living as a transient in Denver, Colorado, where he dabbled in mining. By this time, his fortunes had declined to nothing, and he spent his final days in poverty, staying in cheap lodging houses where he could barely afford a roof over his head and a dirty mattress to lie on.

Al was positively broke, even after making all that big money in Deadwood. Perhaps he should have stayed in Deadwood, because Al's bleak future would soon become very brutal indeed.

The year 1904 would be an unbelievably bad one for both of the Swearengen brothers. On October 2, 1904, Al's twin brother, Lemuel, was viciously attacked after leaving his meat market in Oskaloosa, Iowa. He suffered a blow to the head and was shot four times, yet strangely, he was not robbed of the day's earnings ($200), nor did he die. Lemuel was found unconscious the next day and was taken to Dr. A.J. Coveny, but he remained in a coma-style situation for eight brutal days. The doctor disclosed that "one bullet hit the bridge of his nose, another hit his brow area, a third hit the back of his head and a fourth hit his right temple."[11] Oddly, the police figured that the gun was held point-blank against Lemuel's skull, so the lead didn't have sufficient force to kill him.

Some feel that since Lemuel was Al's twin, it may have actually been a case of mistaken identity, as Al was, for some time, living in Oskaloosa as well. Did an enemy trace him back to his hometown?

Now living in Denver, Al Swearengen was going by the name of Albert Ellis, possibly to avoid detection by enemies or the law. He was not prospering in his mining endeavors and was really down on his luck—literally.

On July 30, 1904, Al was arrested for vagrancy. A couple months later, he was picked up again and taken to the county jail on October 19 on the same charge. Perhaps he would have been better off safely behind bars, because his life came to a mysterious end just a few weeks later.

Just a little over a month after Lemuel was brutally assaulted in Iowa, Al's luck in Colorado came to a brutal, mysterious end. Did the person or persons responsible for assaulting Lemuel (possibly mistaking him for Al) in Oskaloosa discover Al was now living in Denver? Did they read in the newspaper that the man whom they assaulted was Lemuel and not Al? Did this cause them to go on a manhunt for their real target?

On November 15, 1904, Jack Berry and Steve Eaton were walking down Almeda Avenue in Denver when they stumbled upon a grisly sight. The battered corpse of a male was lying face down in the mud and dirt. His bloody hat was found about seventy feet from his body. Police were quickly called to the scene. The mangled body was that of the notorious Al Swearengen from Deadwood, South Dakota, but locals knew him only as a poor, down on his luck miner named Albert Ellis.

His remains were sprawled out near the Denver and Rio Grande Railroad crossing and tracks. (Where Sante Fe Drive is located today.) Coroner William P. Horan was called to the scene, and he discovered that Al had several broken ribs, crushed legs and a fractured skull and had endured head wounds caused by a blunt instrument. In his pocket was an unsent letter to R.T. Wilson, asking him to bring some tobacco to him at the jail. At the time of his mysterious death, all he had on him was a cheap watch, a small knife, a dynamite fuse and a cap.

The death was quickly labeled a train accident. The authorities thought perhaps he was trying to hop a moving train or that he was already on the train and fell off while it was moving. Perhaps no one really cared, as the man was just a poor vagrant, as far as they were concerned.

Another possibility: one month prior to his death, Al was scheduled to testify against a former friend, John Allison, whom Al believed had stolen $45 from him in Eden, Colorado. Would Allison kill his buddy over $45? (About $1,600 in today's money.) Maybe there is much more to that story!

Now, some researchers believe Al was indeed murdered by an unknown assailant or two.

BACK IN OSKALOOSA, AFTER miraculously surviving his 1904 assault, Lemuel's life took a turn for the worse in 1910 after he got tangled up in a dogfight. On July 6, Lemuel and a man named Lincoln Fisher got into a brawl when their dogs began fighting. The men got into a scuffle (Lemuel threw the first punch), and Lemuel fell down, hitting his head on the curb, resulting in his death a week later, on July 13. Fisher was tried for Lemuel's death, with a $5,000 bond hanging over his head. He was more than likely acquitted of any charges.

Handwritten Coroner's Report for Al Swearengen

Date of Death: Nov. 15, 1904, about 6 p.m. Age about 55 years

Place of death: near the Denver & Rio Grande crossing at Almeda Avenue in Denver County, Colorado.

Occupation: Miner

Investigations developed: that the deceased was found lying dead on the railroad tracks. Skull fractured. Ribs on right side broken. Both Legs badly crushed. Was found by Jack Berry & Steve Eaton, 1211 Byers Street, who were going home from the Rocky Mt. yards at 6:15 p.m. What train struck him was unable to be learned or anyone who witnessed the accident. Deceased was a miner and supposed to have been going up in the mountains. Had recently been released from the County jail. Wm. Goun (?) investigated the case. Coroner removed body. Stephen Eaton testified.

Verdict: That the said Albert Ellis came to his death about 6 o'clock p.m. on the Denver & Rio Grande railroad tracks in the city and county of Denver, State of Colorado from injuries received by being struck by or falling from a train of the said Denver & Rio Grande railroad at the time and place above mentioned.

Signed, W.W. Ross, clerk

Jurors: A.A. Johnson, Ian Kelly, John Horan, Thomas Rowlatt, Wm. M. Burns, A.J. Lockbaum

Nothing of valuable, usual clothing, cheap watch, knife, dynamite fuse, and a dynamite cap—turned over.

R.J. Wilson.

Cause of death: Shock and injuries, R.R. accident.

Inquest held: Nov. 17, 1904, 2 p.m.

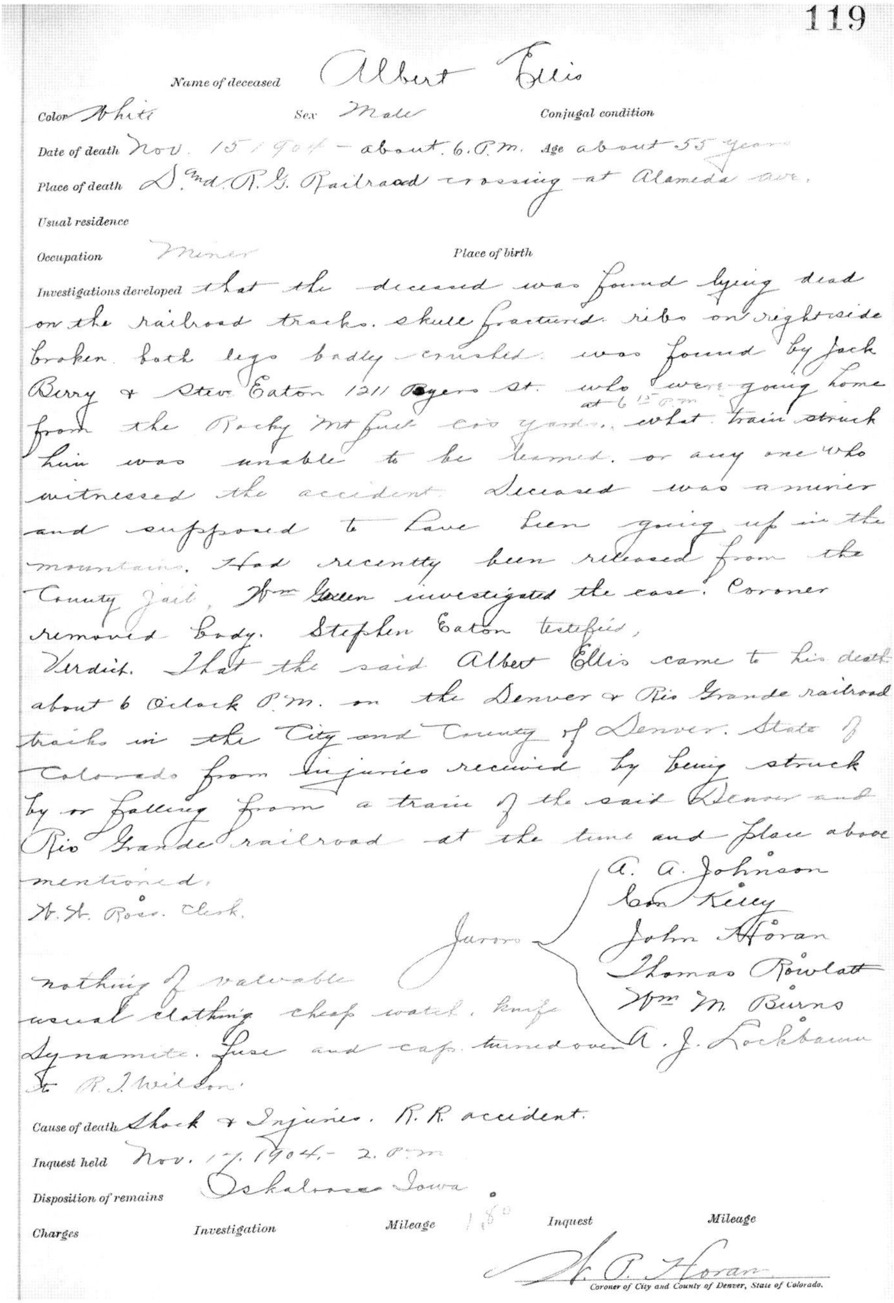

119

Name of deceased Albert Ellis

Color White Sex Male Conjugal condition

Date of death Nov. 15 1904 – about 6. P.m. Age about 55 years

Place of death D. and R. G. Railroad crossing at Alameda ave.

Usual residence

Occupation Miner Place of birth

Investigations developed that the deceased was found lying dead on the railroad tracks. skull fractured. ribs on right side broken. both legs badly crushed. was found by Jack Berry & Steve Eaton 1211 Myers St. who were going home at 6.15 P.m. from the Rocky Mt fuel Cos yards. what train struck him was unable to be learned. or any one who witnessed the accident. Deceased was a miner and supposed to have been going up in the mountains. Had recently been released from the County Jail. Wm Green investigated the case. Coroner removed body. Stephen Eaton testified.

Verdict. That the said Albert Ellis came to his death about 6 Oclock P.m. on the Denver & Rio Grande railroad tracks in the City and County of Denver. State of Colorado from injuries received by being struck by or falling from a train of the said Denver and Rio Grande railroad at the time and place above mentioned.

H. H. Ross. Clerk.

Jurors: A. A. Johnson, Con Kelly, John Horan, Thomas Rowlatt, Wm M. Burns, A. J. Lockbaum

nothing of valuable
usual clothing cheap watch. knife
dynamite. fuse and caps turned over to R. J. Wilson.

Cause of death Shock & Injuries. R. R. accident.

Inquest held Nov. 17. 1904. – 2. P.m

Disposition of remains Oskaloosa Iowa.

Charges Investigation Mileage 1.80 Inquest Mileage

H. P. Horan
Coroner of City and County of Denver, State of Colorado.

Al Swearengen's body was found near Almeda Avenue in Denver, with a fractured skull, broken ribs and crushed legs. His controversial accidental death (or murder) has sparked debate since 1904. The original coroner's report is pictured here. *Courtesy of librarian Alex Hernandez, Denver Public Library Special Collections, WH842.*

Disposition of remains Oskaloosa, Iowa
Mileage 1.80
Signed, W.P. Horan, Coroner of City and County of Denver, State of Colorado[12]

Some questions necessarily come up about Al Swearengen's untimely death as one investigates. If you look at the photo of Al behind his bar in Deadwood (the only known one of two *possible* photographs of him), you'll see he was an extremely heavy man, so unless he lost a lot of weight, it seems unlikely that he was in any condition to jump on or off a moving train. That theory has been tossed aside by many historians anyway, as murder seems more likely. (Or is it simply more exciting than admitting the once rough and tough Al Swearengen died in a clumsy railroad accident?) Or since he was now struggling financially, did he drop a lot of weight prior to his death?

If he really was hit by a train, why didn't the engineer or a brakeman or anyone else who was riding the train at the time notice the accident? Certainly, if the train hit someone hard enough to do all that damage, someone would have noticed. And was blood ever found on the train? No record of a bloody train has been found.

Al had developed a lot of enemies over his lifetime of fifty-nine years: the prostitutes he treated so cruelly, who were begrudgingly making him rich; the three ex-wives he treated just as badly as the whores; the men he sometimes cheated out of their hard-earned money by one means or another. Maybe one of the people he got tangled up with in legal dealings sought revenge? Did any of these people hate Al so much they wanted him dead? Possibly.

Were the killer or killers associates from his Deadwood days or new acquaintances from Denver? Did he get tied up in some difficult matter with his mining claims? He obviously wasn't getting rich working his claim, or else he would have had on better clothes and a nicer watch. And he certainly would not have been picked up for vagrancy two times in the months before his death if he had money.

Where did all his Deadwood money go? If the Gem was making such vast amounts when it was hot, what did Al do with all that money?

Did he really leave Deadwood after all those years simply because the Gem burned down? That seems unlikely, too. Why would he leave a town that was so supportive of his business? Was someone threatening his life in Deadwood, so he decided it was time to beat feet? When Al returned to Deadwood in October 1903 "for good," what prompted him to leave?

Others are certain Al was positively beyond broke at the time of his death and he was trying to hop the train in order to save fare money to get to his mining claim. They believe his injuries were consistent with being hit by a train.

Another possibility is that Al committed suicide by walking in front of a moving train. He had just been arrested a few times for vagrancy, his finances were bleak, his marriages had all failed, he had made a lot of enemies in his life, his mining claim was not producing any income, he had no worldly possessions anymore. Suicide is a definite possibility that has not been addressed.

The now famous Al Swearengen is buried in an unmarked grave near where he grew up at the Forest Cemetery (also known as Forest Memorial Gardens) in Oskaloosa, Mahaska County, Iowa, section 21, lot 14, grave unknown. Al will never know how he came to be a major character in the hit television series *Deadwood*, his life brilliantly portrayed by actor Ian McShane.

A TALENTED DANCER TAKES HER FINAL LEAP

A beautiful and almost famous dancer met her tragic death while living in Deadwood in 1877. Kitty LeRoy (1850–1877, age twenty-seven) traveled all over the United States gracing thousands of spectators with her incredible dancing skills. In 1872, Kitty performed at places like the St. James Theater in Boston, Massachusetts, and was touted as the "lady jig artiste." That same year, she danced in two shows per day while at White's Atheneum on Broadway in New York City. In 1873, she did a three-act drama in Baltimore, Maryland. During the late 1870s, she was dancing onstage in Bay City, Michigan. Somehow, during all this activity, Kitty managed to marry Captain E.H. Lewis (also of Bay City, Michigan). But the couple soon split up after she bore a son to the captain and left Michigan to head west.

In 1876, the *Livingston County Daily Press and Argus* called Kitty the best jig dancer in Saginaw Valley. She even danced her heart away on the stage at Wood's Opera House in Los Angeles, California. She next performed at Bucklies in Virginia City, Nevada, where posters announced her as the best clog dancer around.

Soon Kitty was booked by her agent to perform in Deadwood Gulch. She rolled into town about the same time as some of the most famous pioneers—Wild Bill Hickock and Calamity Jane.

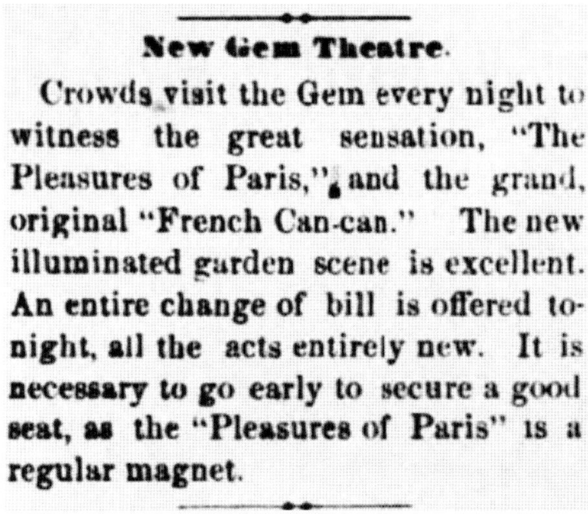

New Gem Theatre.

Crowds visit the Gem every night to witness the great sensation, "The Pleasures of Paris," and the grand, original "French Can-can." The new illuminated garden scene is excellent. An entire change of bill is offered to-night, all the acts entirely new. It is necessary to go early to secure a good seat, as the "Pleasures of Paris" is a regular magnet.

A local newspaper ad placed by Al Swearengen promoting cancan dancers and the suggestive *Pleasures of Paris* theater act. His saloon and theater were crowded every night of the week. *Courtesy of the* Black Hills Pioneer Times, *January 14, 1880.*

Kitty began performing at Al Swearengen's Gem Variety Theatre and the Bella Union in Deadwood, which made both places even more popular with the locals. But when she put down stakes in Deadwood, her life slowly took a turn for the worse. Even though she was still married, Kitty dazzled all the men, and her dance card was always full. She stole the heart of a saloon man named Michael Raymond for a few months, but they split up when she found a new love. A faro dealer named Samuel R. Curley took a shine to Kitty, and the two were married on June 10, 1877, by the justice of the peace in Deadwood. The wedding took place at the Gem Theatre, with Judge Charles Baker officiating, Cliff Sam standing as the best man and Fannie Garretson as the bridesmaid.

But Curley didn't like Kitty dancing at the Gem and demanded she stop performing. Yet without her income, money was tight, so Curley took a job in Cheyenne, Wyoming, as a dealer in a saloon. (Some records indicate that Kitty opened up her own place, called the Mint Gambling Saloon, but that has not been verified.)

While Curley was working in Cheyenne, Kitty's bed got lonely, and she hooked back up with an old lover. When Curley found out his wife was cheating on him, he became furious. He also discovered that she had gotten involved with prostitution, at a house of ill repute upstairs in the Lone Star building on lower Main Street near Chinatown in Deadwood, adding salt to his wound.

Curley had had enough of this monkey business and made his way back to Deadwood to talk some sense into his wife. As he was preparing for his trip, Kitty got word Curley was coming for her, so she borrowed money off her landlord, eager to get out of Deadwood—pronto.

But that fatal night, December 6, Kitty dressed up and got ready to do a favorite dance number one last time—for old times' sake. She tucked her lovely body into a fanciful dress (later called the "Dance of Death" costume). While she was in her room at the Lone Star, completing the finishing touches on her hair and makeup, Curley was downstairs having supper, unknown to Kitty. After he finished his meal, he slowly made his way up the stairs to Kitty's room. Just as she opened the door, Curley pulled out his Smith & Wesson .44 and shot her right in the middle of her torso. He then aimed his gun at his temple and pulled the trigger.

The double crime happened very quickly, and after people heard the gunshots, they gathered upstairs to see what all the commotion was about. There in the hallway lay the bloody corpses of both Kitty and Curley.

The whole town was in shock at the murder/suicide that had just taken place. The mess was cleaned up as best it could be, and the double funeral was performed in the saloon at the Lone Star, with Reverend Norcross saying their final prayers.

The quarrelsome couple was buried at Ingleside Cemetery, but their bodies were later moved to Mount Moriah. The *Black Hills Weekly Times* reported that the ghostly spirits of both Kitty and Curley had been seen in the Lone Star Saloon several times by multiple witnesses.

When alive, Kitty was extremely talented and had a bright future. She claimed to have had five husbands, Curley being her fifth and final. One of her many husbands let her shoot an apple off his head as she quickly rode by on her horse! She had thick brown hair and was both tall and graceful. She bragged about owning seven revolvers and twelve knives, loved to gamble and always wore large diamonds in her delicate ears.

THE GEM'S KITTY CLYDE MURDERED; KILLER THEN SHOOTS HIMSELF

Theresa "Kitty" Clyde (1861–1883, age twenty-one) knew how to draw a crowd and entertain the men at Al Swearengen's Gem Variety Theatre. She sashayed into the Gem all the way from Chicago, Illinois, with her boyfriend, former Deadwood citizen Charles Wilson (1851–1883, age thirty-one). Wilson's father, Calvin G. Wilson (1815–1890, age seventy-five), had become a resident of south Deadwood sometime between 1875 and 1876. One of the town's original pioneers, Calvin "Pap" Wilson was well known and well liked by everyone in the Black Hills. Pap enjoyed fishing and hunting and seemed to defy aging.

Pap's son, Charles, moved back to Deadwood with Kitty in tow, via wagon, in October 1883. She and Charles had decided to head west with Swearengen (when he was returning from one of his trips to secure fresh blood and entertainers for his saloon).

Kitty quickly became known in Deadwood as a fun-loving woman who worked once in a while as a prostitute as well as a dancer and actress. She lived in a house on Van Buren Street in town. Charles was madly in love with her and sought her hand in marriage, but Kitty refused. It was rumored that she was in love with someone else, and besides, it was also rumored that Charles already had a wife in Sioux City.

Charles had a job painting the new school in Deadwood, but he cut out early on the night of the tragedy. He walked home, changed out of his work clothes and then went to town to see if he could find Kitty.

That day, Charles had been drinking heavily. Kitty was working at the Gem, as usual, so it wasn't hard to find her. As Charles continued to fuel his thirst, the booze fueled his jealousy. He marched into the Gem, pointed the pistol right at Kitty's head and pulled the trigger. As she lay bleeding on the floor, he turned the gun toward himself and pulled the trigger a second time. But he did not die instantly, as poor Kitty had.

Marshal Tyler was called to the scene. The bullet had entered the base of Kitty's skull, its trajectory slightly upward, and lodged in her brain. Coroner Smith took her body to the morgue and placed it in an icebox to be held until the funeral. Her good friends in town pooled their money and purchased Kitty's casket. She was dressed in her finest costume and laid to rest at Mount Moriah Cemetery.

Charles lingered in complete agony for several days. His bullet had entered his right temple and destroyed his eye. The doctor tried to remove the bullet while the patient was under the effects of chloroform, but the bullet would remain forever lodged behind the killer's left eye.

Some felt it served him right. His father, Calvin, tried to comfort his son in the small cabin he lived in. Doctors could do nothing to save Charles, and he died on November 17 at 4:00 p.m. His funeral was held at B.P. Smith's Undertaking. He was also buried at Mount Moriah Cemetery in Deadwood.

Calvin "Pap" Wilson never mentally recovered from his son's murderous revenge and suicide. His health slowly declined, and in early January 1890, he suffered from a paralytic stroke. On his deathbed, he gave his favorite dog, Pop, to his good friend Miss Eva Chiniquy. Pop remained restless after Pap's death, and he continued to roam the streets of Deadwood in search of his master.

> NOTE: Calvin Wilson was also one of the first people to witness the crime scene of the murder of Winnie Callison on August 19, 1878 (see the story "Killed Over a Secret" on page 76).

A GEM PROSTITUTE AND A KNIFE

Gertie Moss was working as a prostitute at the Gem Theatre, along with Annie Ford. A disagreement broke out between the two soiled doves, and Gertie pulled out a large knife and slashed Ford with it.

Gertie was arrested and put away in jail. Deadwood Deputy Sheriff W.P. Tyler filed a formal complaint against Gertie on April 19, 1884, charging her with assault with a dangerous weapon with the intent to do bodily harm. Gertie found herself with a hefty $300 bail bond hanging over her head. Gertie requested a continuance, and the trial was moved to May 5.

Luckily, Annie was able to survive her slashing.

On the date of the trial, Gertie was nowhere to be found. Rumor had it she hopped aboard the Sydney Coach and fled Deadwood for good.

Annie had arrived in Deadwood on July 19, 1881, from Bell Fourche and taken up residence at the Wentworth House. She eventually found employment at the Gem as a "sporting girl." In 1884, a patron of Annie's stole her watch, and charges were filed. The judge decided there was not enough evidence to prosecute the man.

But Annie's luck would eventually change, and on January 13, 1887, three years after Gertie's attack, Annie was happily married to Mr. Bird Rose by Father Walsh, and the two held a grand wedding in town. Over one hundred people showed up to celebrate and eat a hearty supper with the new couple. The Roses were well liked and well respected in Deadwood.

A close-call slashing could have turned into a full-blown murder if Annie did not survive the horrible ordeal.

Where Gertie Moss ended up remains a mystery. She probably changed her name and took up elsewhere in another state.

Banjo Dick Shoots Shaughnessy at the Bella Union

Deadwood was known for being a madhouse at times, and the evening of November 16, 1876, was one of those times.

The night started out a good one. Mr. and Mrs. Richard "Banjo Dick" Brown (Mrs. Brown was really Fannie Garretson) were performing onstage, delighting all who listened with their music. The crowd was having a wonderful time, and the gaiety in the saloon was infectious—that is, until a man named Edward Shaughnessy walked through its doors.

Apparently in a bad and jealous mood, Shaughnessy threw an axe at the musicians and then tried to crawl up onto the stage. The entertainers were scared half to death, so Brown quickly grabbed his gun and shot back at the madman, fearing for their lives. "He has followed me enough!" Brown yelled out.[13] Three times he pulled the trigger, and all three bullets went into Shaughnessy's body.

Shaughnessy died in the morning. Brown was arrested, tried and acquitted on grounds of self-defense. But Shaughnessy's tragic story actually started the year before.

Earlier, a variety troupe came to Deadwood to perform at the Bella Union Theater, run by Billy Nuttall and Tom Miller. Fannie Garretson also came to Deadwood from Cheyenne, Wyoming, that year to perform at the Bella Union. Prior to that, she'd fallen in love with a Union Pacific railroad man named Ed Shaughnessy, and they got married and lived at various places along the Union Pacific route. (Later, on December 30, 1876, Fannie posted a notice in the *Black Hills Weekly Pioneer* that she had only *lived* with Shaughnessy; they were never legally married.) They eventually broke up when Fannie fell in love with Dick Brown, and Fannie and Dick started to perform music shows together. As soon as they arrived in Deadwood, they tied the knot (rumors claimed that Fannie was still married to Ed), very much in love. A quick ceremony by Mayor Farnum and it was official. "Free drinks for all!" Brown called to the happy crowd at the Gem.[14]

Shaughnessy did not take the breakup well, and once he found out his wife was in Deadwood, he came looking for her. He also threatened to kill Brown multiple times, and it was noted that Shaughnessy made countless death threats against Brown in front of witnesses.

Billy Nuttall and Tom Miller had agreed to not allow Shaughnessy into their establishment for everyone's safety.

But on the night of November 16, Shaughnessy cleverly had someone else buy him a ticket to get in. He sat by the stove near the stage, waiting for

Energetic and fascinating dancers graced the stage nightly at the Gem, making it the hottest spot to enjoy a wild evening in Deadwood. *Courtesy of LOC#2014636781, woman dancing and performing acrobatics, United States Printing Company, 1898.*

an opportunity. When "Banjo Dick" and Fannie Garretson-Brown started singing a duet, Shaughnessy's jealousy went wild. When the duo finished their number and started kissing and hugging, Shaughnessy lost his mind. The axe was thrown at Brown, and Brown quickly grabbed his gun. Then shots were fired at Shaughnessy.

Shaughnessy was taken to the Grand Central Hotel, where he died at 5:00 p.m. on November 17. Brown told the jury that he attacked Shaughnessy on the spur of the moment. Everyone agreed that Brown was defending himself and his new bride. The jury found Dick Brown not guilty, he was acquitted of murder and the case was closed.

Brown later partnered with Billy Nuttal and opened a spot in the Melodeon Building.

For some reason, Fannie attempted to slit her own throat with a razor but recovered.

Having had enough drama, Brown placed an ad in the *Black Hills Daily Times* on August 11, 1877:

For Sale. One cabin on two lots, bed, mattress, table, mirror, etc., etc., the whole business. $50. AM GOING AWAY. Dick Brown.

In 1880, Fannie left Deadwood and moved to Leadville, Colorado.

"Banjo Dick" Brown moved to Pensacola, Florida.

It is unknown whether the couple ever officially divorced. Reports in the *Dodge City Globe* on July 30, 1878, have the couple singing and performing together back onstage in Dodge City, Kansas, with the troupe Comique along with a woman named Fannie Keenan. Keenan was shot and killed while rooming with Garretson on October 5, 1878.

THE UNSOLVED MURDER OF BILLY BIRD

On July 4, 1881, the battered body of a local Deadwood man named Billy Bird was found on Spring Creek Road near the hospital. Officials were called, and Coroner Smith came to the scene. He examined Bird and discovered a wound on the side of his head. Bird's clothes were soaking wet, and a large stone was lying near his body with blood and hair on it. He had been stabbed so violently that a piece of the knife was lodged in his skull.

Earlier that day, a Mr. Burnham had seen Billy Bird sitting on a rock with his clothes covered in blood. He thought Bird had suffered a possible concussion from a fall or something of that nature. Burnham ran to get help, but when he returned, Billy Bird was dead.

Billy Bird had no enemies. He was slightly mentally incapacitated but harmless. He had come to Deadwood, where his brother worked at the Bank Saloon, from Whitewater, Wisconsin. Billy had been working at a wagon-making company and dabbling in blacksmithing at Patton's Stable on Wall Street in town where Henry Strang was the manager.

Billy Bird's killer was never apprehended, and his horrible death would go without justice—yet another Deadwood murder left unsolved forever.

Billy Bird, a local blacksmith working at Patton's stables, was brutally attacked and killed in 1881. Part of the assassin's knife was lodged in his skull. His murderer was never found. *Courtesy of the* Black Hills Weekly Pioneer, *July 9, 1879.*

Mr. Tuttle Killed in Treasure Gulch

Greed and the lure of gold have taken many lives over the years. On September 5, 1887, an unsettled dispute over a mining claim caused violence and death in Treasure Gulch.

Mr. J.C. Tuttle would take his last breath as he was trying to repair a wheelbarrow in Treasure Gulch, between Blacktail Gulch and Sawpit Gulch, just outside of Deadwood. The shot was fired by an unknown assailant from the rear of a nearby cabin. The bullet lodged in Tuttle's lower abdomen, but he did not die instantly; the Grim Reaper took a few days.

Tuttle was a hardworking man who owned one-third interest in the Aurora Mine. After he was shot, he described what happened:

> *I was greasing a wheel-barrow on Aurora mining ground when shot. I don't know where the shot came from that hit me. I was not resisting anyone. I had a revolver in my pocket but did not show any firearms. I don't know how many shots were fired. I told one of the Keet's men that if I was badly off to go get a pistol and come out and I would satisfy him alone. This was all that passed between me and the Keet's men. It was*

> *about fifteen minutes from the time of my telling the man to get a pistol before the shooting commenced.*[15]

To try to keep the peace, the men from both mines, the Aurora Mine and the Keets Mine, had all entered into a legal agreement on August 16, 1877, that made it clear they would not interfere with each other and that no more ore would be removed from the Aurora Mine until a new survey was conducted. This agreement was signed by Alvin Whitney and M.E. Post of the Keets Mining Company and J. Cephas Tuttle, C.H. Detrick and Thomas Platt of the Aurora Mining Company.

The Keets men were a band of forty-plus men who were part of the Keets Company. They were angry at Tuttle and had taken possession of a tunnel in the Aurora Mine the night prior to his murder. (This tunnel connected the Aurora Mine to the Keets Mine.) After the Keets men went through the process of putting miscellaneous items in the shaft to obstruct it, an equally angry and frustrated Tuttle took it upon himself to blow out the shaft.

James Johnson was at the crime scene and later recalled what he saw happen. "I saw a number of shots fired at the Aurora cabin. I saw Mr. Tuttle walking from the shaft of the Aroura Mine towards a wheelbarrow. He appeared to be repairing it. Then I heard a single shot and saw gun smoke coming from the rear of the Keet's cabin. Mr. Tuttle then fell to the ground."[16]

Coroner S.F. Babcock was soon on the scene, along with Sheriff Seth Bullock. The calm, cool and always collected Bullock arrested George Fullerton, J.S. Hubbard, Joe Maxwell, C.L. Torbet, J.S. Goddard, E.C. Smith and H.T. Paslin in connection with Tuttle's murder.

An inquest into the murder was organized in the Bella Union Theater on September 8. (Those attending the trial also got a free variety show, as the entertainers were rehearsing their parts in a nearby room at the Bella Union.) It was determined that Tuttle was simply defending his own land, but no one was ever convicted of his murder. All the Keets men claimed their innocence (most were on the board of the Keets Mining Company, which protected them).

Tuttle's death would forever go down in history as an unsolved murder in Deadwood.

A Spoiled Teen and a Bad Temper

I have to say gentlemen here, that I was fetched here by my own fault. I don't know what is the reason, but when I was small, I always had a bad temper. I was not such a wayward child, but I was born with a desire to ramble all the time. Before my mother died, I think I was a good child in everything. She died when I was young; and after that I did not appear to have much pleasure at home. My father was a man willing, perhaps, to do everything to take care of me, but I wanted to wander away from home and left home three or four times, and my father fetched me back, and I went to California. Still my heart has not been bad.

—James Leighton Gilmore, 1882,
right before his execution on the scaffold[17]

It seemed James Leighton Gilmore was in trouble from the day he was born in 1858. His father was a policeman in Steubenville, Ohio, where they lived. The rebellious Gilmore just couldn't behave. He was constantly disappointing his dad by committing arson, stealing horses and running away from home. His family was fairly wealthy, so there was no real need for the teenager to commit such reckless actions.

During the summer of 1879, Gilmore was working as a driver of mules and oxen. Somewhere between Fort Pierce and Deadwood, Gilmore ran into a Hispanic bullwhacker (a person who drove an oxen- or mule-drawn freight wagon using a very long whip to direct and control their animals) named Clementi (also Bicente) Ortes (also Ortez) on the trail. Both men had stopped for the night at a spot called Dead Man's Creek. Gilmore started unhitching his team of cattle and oxen. He did not like the way Ortes was causing his team to become nervous.

"I will beef you as soon as I get these cattle unyoked!" he yelled to Ortes, and after he unhitched his team, he went to grab his revolver. Ortes just stood on the trail, watching Gilmore.[18]

"Defend yourself!" Gilmore yelled to Ortes. But before Ortes could even grab his gun, Gilmore shot him twice. One bullet hit Ortes's left arm, and the other passed through him and out his back.

Without a care in the world, Gilmore left Ortes for dead and went to sleep for the night.

At about nine o'clock the next morning, as Gilmore was heading back out toward Fort Pierre, he noticed Ortes was dead, but he could not have cared less. Gilmore spent a few days in Pierre and then made his way to Yankton, where he met with a man with the Rosebud Agency, seeking employment to drive mules for the government. He stopped for a bite to eat at a saloon between Three Mile Ranch and Hog Ranch.

After Ortes's body was found, Gilmore was arrested by Deputy Marshal Grey and taken to Deadwood for a trial.

"Is this for killing that damn Mexican? That was an accident. I only intended to wing him," Gilmore told Grey. He also told Grey that Ortes had had a large knife and threatened to kill him with it.

Neither Grey nor the judge nor the jury believed Gilmore's story of self-defense. Twenty-four-year-old Gilmore was sentenced to hang for the crime, and his execution was scheduled. His would go down in history as the first local, *legal* execution in the Black Hills.

Gilmore's family tried in vain to save him from the gallows and to get his sentence reduced to life in prison instead. They rallied as many people as they could to try to get Gilmore off the hook. Appeals were filed, one after the other. Letters were written emphasizing that "his brother was a popular naval officer." Opinions started to change a little bit when important citizens started begging for mercy: the Secretary of the Navy, George Maxwell Robeson; Senator John Percival Jones of Nevada; and even Nevada Governor John Henry Kinkaid pleaded for a lighter sentence for Gilmore. Governor N.G. Ordway of the Dakota Territory issued an order reprieving Gilmore for ten days, which stayed the execution.

But after many failed attempts, the hanging was scheduled, and Gilmore was finally dropped at 2:45 p.m. on December 15, 1882, at the first Lawrence County jail (built in 1877, a wooden thirty-by-fifty-foot structure). Al Raymond, chief deputy United States marshal, was in charge. Gilmore's body was taken down by Coroner Smith and buried on December 19 at Mount Moriah Cemetery.

In 2006, the Deadwood Historic Preservation Commission had a grave marker put at Gilmore's gravesite.

CHIEF TWO STICKS HANGED

Chief Two Sticks, named Cha Nopa Uhah by his tribe, was a strong Lakota Sioux warrior who was sometimes considered brutal and ruthless.

In 1894, after decades of Lakota leadership, the reign of Chief Two Sticks would come to a painful end. Some in his band were accused of massacring several of Humphrey and Stenger's working cowboys at the

Isaac Humphrey Ranch. At one point, the army pretended that Two Sticks and his men were responsible for stealing cattle owned by white ranchers. Another battle soon developed, this one leaving five police officers killed, but Two Sticks and others in his band escaped. There would be more battles and more deaths.

Chief Two Sticks was arrested by Deputy United States Marshals Matthiessen and Jarchow in connection with the incidents. Two Sticks had obviously been shot and injured prior to his apprehension. The doctors feared his arm was gangrenous, requiring amputation, but Two Sticks refused help. At over seventy years old, he chose to suffer in jail without medical aid. The gangrene painfully moved into his shoulder. His son Marks and his nephew were also in jail alongside him, praying for his health.

Tragically, on December 28, 1894, the once powerful Chief Two Sticks was hanged in Deadwood. The gallows were built in the space between the jail and the horse stable. Over two hundred people attended the execution. Right before the trap was to be released, Two Sticks raised both his hands and sang a sorrowful death song. His final words were, "My heart knows I am not guilty, and I am happy. I am not afraid to die. I was taught that if I raised my hands to Wakan Tanka [God] and told a lie, that God would kill me that day. I never told a lie in my life."[19]

The body of Two Sticks was placed in a pine coffin and taken to Smith's Undertaking. His old white felt hat was given to Sheriff Remer. Chief Two Sticks' final resting place remains an eternal mystery.

Emma Stone Bludgeoned in Her Sleep

The horrific murder of Mrs. Emma Stone (1846–1897, age fifty) in 1897 was shocking to everyone. It was considered one of the most cold-blooded killings ever witnessed in Deadwood.

On Saturday, May 14, 1897, Mrs. Stone was found at six o'clock in the morning by Maggie Hudson, dead in her bedroom (which was next to the Syndicate Restaurant). Her head had nearly been cut off by a heavy butcher's cleaver. Was it just burglary? Rage? The room was in disarray, and blood was everywhere.

Dr. Paddock arrived at the scene around 6:10 a.m. and determined that Emma had been dead for about four hours (which put the time of her murder around 2:00 a.m.) Her gold watch, gold chain and gold ring had all been stolen from her body. The Stones were productive, hardworking and

Left: In 1897, Emma Stone was brutally murdered in her sleep by an intoxicated Charles Brown (real name Isador Cavanaugh), the cook in her family's restaurant on lower Main Street in Deadwood. *Courtesy of the* Deadwood Evening Independent, *July 14, 1897.*

Right: One of Emma Stone's advertisements ran in the local newspapers promoting her family's hotel, twenty-four-hour restaurant and pool hall. Emma would later be bludgeoned to death in her back bedroom. *Courtesy of the* Daily Deadwood Pioneer-Times, *March 9, 1881.*

well-liked people in Deadwood, and Emma's brutal murder left everyone in complete panic and shock. Who in the world would do such a thing?

Emma Frances Hukill Stone was born in Cincinnati, Ohio, on April 3, 1846. She studied at Wesleyan Female College, also in Cincinnati. On October 5, 1864, she married Colonel Lewis P. Stone (1843–1903, age sixty) in Hamilton County, Ohio. The couple had one beautiful daughter, Bessie (1872–1912, age forty). They came to Deadwood in 1876 in the hopes of starting a new life together in the beautiful Black Hills. They'd heard of the gold rush and were eager to benefit from its bounty. They opened a successful restaurant and a small boardinghouse located on lower Main Street.

After some investigation, the prime suspect was identified as the restaurant's very own cook, Charles Brown. The authorities found the killer hanging out in Whitewood at Jesse Walker's residence, and after questioning Brown, Sheriff Plunkett and Deputy Lackous arrested him. After a few weeks of contemplation, Brown confessed to the savage killing. He told officials the tragic story in great detail.

The night of the murder, Brown and a young man, Ralph Walker, decided to start drinking. After a bit, the two got hungry, so Brown suggested they go to his workplace, where he could make them supper—but first, more drinking. They went into Simpson's Saloon and then wandered around Chinatown for a bit before heading back to the Stones' Hotel and Restaurant (some records state it was called the Keystone Restaurant) around one o'clock in the morning, where Walker fell asleep on a cot in the hallway.

After a bit, Walker was awakened by a frantic and sweaty Brown. He indicated Walker should get up and get dressed. The men walked down the Elkhorn railroad tracks to a friend's house on lower Main Street. Brown looked at Walker and threatened to kill him if he told anyone about anything.

Now in jail, Brown knew he was not getting out. He told the officers that his real name was Isador Cavanaugh and that he knew Emma Stone kept her money and gold between her mattresses. He was drunk that night, and he wanted to rob her. He tried to break into her trunk, but her small dog started barking. When Mrs. Stone woke up, he panicked and hit her with a meat cleaver—but he meant to kill the dog, he said, not Mrs. Stone. Brown said he buried the stolen items in an old barn in Crook City before he was arrested and that he was planning on giving Emma's gold watch to Mrs. Jesse Walters.

On June 10, the twelve-man jury deliberated for only twelve minutes, and the conclusion they came to for Judge Plowman was that Brown was definitely guilty of cold-blooded murder.

Brown was put on death watch (to make sure the prisoner didn't commit suicide before the execution took place), and he casually smoked a free cigar. His last meal request on July 14 was a simple plate of eggs and toast, along with corned beef and cabbage. At 9:00 a.m., he was read his death warrant. At 10:22 a.m., he was walked up the scaffolding alongside Father Burke, where his death noose swung, waiting to secure its hold around his neck.

When asked if he had any final words, Brown replied, "I have faith in the Lord Jesus Christ. I have admitted to man and God that I killed Emma Frances Stone. I am sorry for it and ask God to forgive me. Goodbye to the world."[20]

Emma's distraught husband, Colonel Stone, wanted to be the one to actually pull the lever on the scaffold, causing the warranted death of the man who murdered his beloved wife, but his friends and family talked him out of it. The lever was pulled, and the trapdoor opened under Brown's feet. Brown dropped the required eight and a half feet—but his strong neck did not break. A man in the crowd reportedly said, "His infernal neck is as hard as his heart; it wouldn't break!"[21]

Brown hung strangling from the rope for a long, torturous twenty-three minutes before he was finally pronounced dead. No one seemed to care or feel bad about the botched execution. After all, justice is justice.

Isador Cavanaugh (also known as Charles Brown) was born on March 1, 1843, on a slave farm owned by Colonel Halliday near Macon City, Missouri. His parents were both slaves of Halliday's. His mother died when he was nine years old. Brown was sold to another slave owner. He suffered no physical or sexual abuse from any of his owners. He was then sold to a slave owner named Cavanaugh (this is where he got the new last name). Cavanaugh set him free, and for the next few years, Brown worked odd jobs in places like New York City, Chicago, New Orleans and various towns in Texas. He came to the Black Hills in 1879 and settled in at Deadwood just before the 1896 fire. Just one year later, he would be hanged for murder.

It was reported that a Chinese woman viewed his body after his execution, and her grief was intense. Her identity remains unknown.

> Note: Both Colonel Stone and Emma are buried at Mount Moriah Cemetery in Deadwood, section 2, lot 75. Their daughter Bessie married Michael D. Rossiter (1857–1948, age ninety-one) in 1898, and the couple eventually moved to California.

The Death of China Doll

One of the more bizarre unsolved murders in Deadwood's history is the killing of a beautiful and rich woman named Di Lee. Her background was incredibly mysterious, and it was said her beauty was so extreme that any man who gazed upon her would be driven insane by thoughts of love and passion. Many men believed that Di Lee (also known as China Doll) was like a living picture; her smile would melt even a heart of granite.

But there was obviously someone who was not in awe of her beauty: the people who viciously attacked and brutally killed her.

Di Lee was one of the first Chinese women to arrive in Deadwood, in 1876. She was so wealthy that she immediately purchased three homes in town and several lots on Main Street. She also owned property in Denver, Colorado. In the 1870s, women did not usually own property without the help of a man, so where did Di Lee get all her money? She was not a prostitute. She was not married. Was she a princess? Everyone wondered. Some even speculated that Di Lee was a personal slave to a wealthy Mongolian man in California.

On the night of November 27, 1877, two unknown assailants pounced on Di Lee. They hit her beautiful face with a hatchet and inflicted multiple stab wounds into her back with a knife. She was not robbed, as her valuables were found in her room and a fancy bracelet, although loosened, was still on her slender wrist.

Passerby Sam Loy, a Chinese man, stumbled upon the grisly scene and notified a night watchman at ten o'clock. Di Lee's body was found in one of her cabins in upper Chinatown. The police found that her bracelet, worth sixty dollars, had been partially pulled from her wrist—was it wanted as a token of the killing or proof that it had been committed by those who ordered the hit? Her home showed obvious evidence of a violent struggle: there was blood all over the walls and floors. A bloody handprint was stamped over Di Lee's mouth: an attempt to stifle her screams or a grisly reminder that some people need to remain silent?

It was known that the girls at the Bella Union were extremely jealous of Di Lee, for none of them could compete with her beauty, and she did not have to sell her body to strangers in order to live her extravagant lifestyle.

At Di Lee's funeral, her body was surrounded by many candles and perfumed papers, as was Chinese tradition. She was buried two days later. Some locals claim that Di Lee's restless spirit returned to her home and repeated, "*Moo shoot nghin!*"—"Do not kill me!"[22]

Locals Ah Sing and his wife were arrested on suspicion of Di Lee's murder on December 3, but nothing came of it. Ah Hem and his wife, Ark Hem, were also arrested and questioned on December 4, but they were released for lack of evidence as well.

Deadwood coroner Charles Meyer reported that the multiple stab wounds did not cause Di Lee's death, but the two massive blows to her head caused serious fractures, and they were what caused her demise.

Di Lee may have been buried in Ingleside Cemetery (Deadwood's original cemetery, now houses), but the location of her gravesite is unknown. Why?

There was a secret society in Deadwood's Chinatown called the Tongs. During that time, it controlled the area and other gangs. Did they have anything to do with Di Lee's murder? If so, why?

Deadwood's Chinatown had its own unofficial mayor and council. They took matters (and punishments) into their own hands. They also had their own private groups of police and firemen to protect Chinatown.

The bodies of the Chinese deceased were sometimes exhumed and sent back to China to be reburied. The Chinese often signed contracts with the companies that brought them to the United States for employment stipulating that on their deaths, their bodies would be sent back to China. So if they were buried before the request for their return, undertakers would be obligated to carefully dig them up, box up the corpse and send their body back to their homeland.

The actual whereabouts of Di Lee's murdered body remain a dark and mysterious chapter in Deadwood's history.

Deadwood Doctor Beaten

Deadwood's local Dr. Patrick T. Connolly (1827?–1889, age approximately sixty-two) suspiciously dropped dead in Jacob Schubert's Saloon on Main Street at 7:30 a.m. on May 10, 1889.

The night before, around midnight, Bill Dunn had bumped into Dr. Connolly, and they chatted about nothing in particular. Then Connolly, oddly, said, "I'm going home. I am going to die like Pembroke B. Stearns did."[23] (Stearns had died a week earlier from heart disease.)

Earlier that morning, Dr. Connolly was seen loitering around Phillips & Burroughs Drug Store then walking awkwardly down the street to lower Main, where he entered Schubert's Saloon and fell to the floor.

The bartender, L.H. Edding, later said, "The doctor came into Schubert's Saloon about 7:30 a.m. He staggered the length of the bar then fell on his hands and knees and rolled over onto his back. I raised him into a sitting position then got him into a chair. 'Do you want a beer?' I asked him."[24] The doctor looked at Edding and said, "Yes," but he didn't take the beer. Instead, he threw his blood-soaked hat on the table.[25]

Dr. Rogers was called to administer help to poor Dr. Connolly. Dr. Baker also rushed to help, but when he arrived, he told everyone that Connolly was, unfortunately, beyond help. Connolly died thirty minutes later. Rogers cleaned up Connolly's head to assess where the blood was coming from. He announced, "Death came by cuts and abrasions on top of the head, the heavy blows causing injury to the brain."[26]

When Connolly was inspected further, it was discovered that he had two large, deep gashes on the top of his head caused by a blunt object. The doctors believed that the wounds were approximately four hours old.

Deadwood in 1888 as seen from McGovern Hill. That year, the new Deadwood Street Railway, a horse-drawn trolley system, ran one and a half miles along Main, Lee and Sherman Streets. *Courtesy of LOC# 99613870, John C.H. Grabill, photographer.*

Locals told the doctors that they'd noticed Connolly had been ill for the past few days, was not acting normally and seemed extremely nervous.

Later, James Ryan found a woman's apron in the bushes on a path that led to Connolly's cabin. It was covered in fresh blood. A small sack of coffee beans was also found nearby. Was the blood human or from a butchered chicken? Did the bloody apron even have anything to do with Connolly's murder? Who knows.

Connolly's funeral was held at the Catholic cemetery in Deadwood.

Patrick Connolly had migrated from Canada, where he graduated from McGill Medical College in Montreal. He was considered one of the best surgeons in the United States.

Dr. Connolly came to Deadwood in 1876 during the gold rush era and practiced medicine in the rough-and-tumble town. Soon he was well-known as an excellent physician to all the locals. Everyone loved him! Well, everyone except one person…

His unsolved murder was definitely the result of foul play, and his killer was never apprehended.

The $220 Murder

The idea of killing someone over a small amount of money sounds insane, but it happens every day. Things were no different in 1878.

Chris Hoffman ran the Hoffman Saloon in Deadwood on Main Street. Originally from Cheyenne, Wyoming, he enjoyed the locals and had a good reputation in town. But he owed Ed Durham money, and he couldn't pay up.

The unsolved debt turned into murder when Durham showed up at Hoffman's saloon, the Progressive Hall, on April 28, 1878, at about four o'clock in the afternoon. Durham waltzed into the bar, pulled his pistol from its holster and fired at Hoffman. Three shots rang through the air for everyone to hear, wounding Hoffman. Hoffman, seeking refuge, ran out of the saloon and into a barbershop adjacent to his building. Durham chased him into the barbershop, aimed his pistol and tried to fire again, but all three times, the gun misfired.

Frustrated, Durham ran away up Lee Street toward Williams Street, trying to escape, but concerned citizens and officers were hot on his trail. "Halt!" yelled a policeman, but Durham kept running.

In 1878, Ed Durham was sentenced to twenty-one years' hard labor at the Detroit House of Corrections (pictured) for killing Chris Hoffman over $220. He was set free after only six years, never to be seen again. *Courtesy of LOC #2016802083, Detroit Publishing Company, Michigan.*

Pat McHugh was having no part of this nonsense. He pulled out his own gun and pointed it at Durham, who quickly surrendered. Officer Mahan apprehended the man and handcuffed him. "*Go to hell!* He owes me $220!" Durham yelled out.[27] (He later claimed it was $1,100 that he was owed.)

In the meantime, Hoffman died.

Durham was tried for Hoffman's murder. The jury rendered a verdict of manslaughter in the first degree on June 19, 1878, and Durham was sentenced by Judge Barnes to twenty-one years' hard labor. He was taken away to the house of corrections in Detroit, Michigan.

But "hard labor" in the Detroit House of Corrections wasn't so hard after all, and it was reported that Durham was getting fat and enjoying life in prison.

In 1884, just six short years into Durham's twenty-one-year sentence, Governor N.G. Ordway pardoned him. Maybe the state decided that housing and feeding big ol' Durham for another fifteen years wasn't worth the cost. Either way, Durham was never seen or heard from again.

A Prank Goes Awry

Lloyd Webster Forbes (1856–1878, age twenty-one) purchased a profitable quartz mill in the Black Hills. Forbes was a very well-connected young man and grew up in a rather privileged, wealthy home. The Forbes family had servants and butlers and not a care in the world, really.

William "Bill" Gay (1844–1876, age thirty-two, after whom the town of Gayville, near Deadwood, is named) lived most of his life among the Sioux Indians and knew the Black Hills like the back of his hand. He became a cowboy when he was just fourteen years old and later amassed around $100,000 from his gold-mining claim called Blacktail, located two miles above Deadwood (he owned one of the very first local quartz mines).

Gay and his brother, Al Gay, decided to cash in on the people coming to the area to make more money. Within the small town they created, Bill Gay operated a saloon and gambling hall. He was known to give the shirt off his back to anyone if they were in need.

Late one night, young Lloyd Forbes gave one of the brothers' helpers, a man called General Field, a note to give to Bill Gay's wife, thinking it would be funny to rile up old man Bill. The note read: **Darling, I would like to meet you in the moonlight...alone.**

Gayville, near Deadwood (pictured in 1877), the site of the brutal murder of Lloyd Forbes, age twenty-one, by jealous husband Bill Gay. Gay was pardoned after just one year in jail. *Courtesy of Wikimedia Commons, by Stanley Julius Morrow, public domain.*

The note was supposed to be delivered to Gay's wife, but it was, oddly, given to Mr. Gay instead. After Bill read the note, he was furious with jealousy, determined to confront Forbes about flirting with his wife. He mounted his horse and galloped all the way to Forbes's home. There, he pulled out his pistol and aimed it at Forbes. The young man tried to explain it was just a joke, but Bill Gay, feeling furious, shot him. Forbes died twenty hours later from the gunshot wound to his head. Gay claimed he hit Forbes over the head with his gun and it accidentally discharged. The bullet passed behind Forbes's right ear, fractured his skull and lodged in his brain. (It was later rumored that Forbes was, indeed, Gay's wife's lover.)

Forbes's body was taken from the back of the Carter residence, just one hundred yards from where he was shot, and, later, buried in Mount Moriah Cemetery. He rests eternally next to his brother, J.S. Forbes. His only living relative was Mrs. J.S. Forbes, in Canada. A four-by-eight-foot tomb was built, and Forbes was laid to rest in a metallic rosewood coffin with silver trim and the words **Lloyd Webster Forbes, age 21 years** inscribed on it.

Gay was arrested for Forbes's murder, and bail was set at $7,500. The verdict, read on June 19, 1878, determined that Bill Gay was guilty of manslaughter in the second degree. He was sentenced to fifteen years' hard labor in the house of corrections in Detroit, Michigan.

The citizens of Deadwood and Gayville went to great lengths get Gay released, writing letters and starting petitions begging for his mercy. Their tactics obviously worked, because Governor Howard later pardoned Gay after just one year in jail, due to his rapidly declining health. When Gay arrived back in Gayville, a celebration party was waiting for him.

A GAME OF CARDS LEADS TO MURDER

Several bored young men were sitting around the Vincellette Ranch, about eight miles from Deadwood, playing a game of cards together. Gathered about the dusty table were brothers Azarius and Arsidas Vincellette, Ed Thurlow (age twenty) and Alfred Carroll (age nineteen). They were playing a fairly easy card game called Seven Up. But Thurlow and Carroll soon got into a heated argument and Carroll demanded to take it outside and fight it out, with the Vincellette boys in tow to watch the fun.

It was March 23, 1892, so the weather was still pretty chilly. After a few rounds of punching and cussing, the Vincellette boys got cold and bored and went back inside to resume their card game. It wasn't long before Thurlow appeared at the door with what looked like a broken arm and fell to the ground. Carroll also rushed back into the house, panting and sweating. The boys tried to get Thurlow up but couldn't. They asked Carroll for help.

"Let the son of a bitch die!" he said and turned to leave.[28] Outside, he mounted his horse and rode off back toward his home, about a half mile away.

Thurlow gradually became weaker, and the Vincellette boys grew concerned when they saw all the blood. Frightened, they ran to get their parents, who were upstairs sleeping. Unfortunately, Thurlow died before the parents could even get dressed and come downstairs. He had been stabbed five times.

The parents quickly examined Thurlow and discovered that he had a deep gash on his right shoulder near the collarbone. It was later determined that the stab was so deep it had severed his subclavian artery (a crucial blood vessel situated below the collarbone that's responsible for supplying blood to the upper body, including the head, neck and arms).

Desperate to help Thurlow, Mr. Vincellette hopped on his own horse and galloped two miles away to the Cliff house, where there was a telephone. There he called Sheriff McDonald of Deadwood and told him what had happened.

Carroll, now back at his own house, told his brother that he had stuck Thurlow a good one. Carroll thought it would be best if he left town for a while, so he headed toward Bell Fourche (pronounced *bel-FOOSH*).

The sheriff rode out in the direction of Carroll's house, but he was two hours behind him. He knew Carroll was a horse thief and a known fighter—he had already been in jail several times.

Later, the story surfaced that Carroll *had* been cheating at the card game and that Thurlow tried to shrug it off because he did not think there was any use fighting over a social game of cards.

At 4:00 p.m., Sheriff McDonald reached Bell Fourche, where he traded out his horse for a fresh one. There was already a one-hundred-dollar reward for Carroll's capture, but his trail was cold.

Carroll was busy drinking in a saloon in Deadwood and spoke readily with the local sheriff (he did not know he was the sheriff). The two even ate supper at the Gillmore Hotel later that evening, enjoying a meal at the same table.

But Carroll had drunk too much whiskey and began running his mouth.

When questioned about the recent murder, "Thomas" Carroll told the sheriff that Alfred Carroll was his cousin and he knew the story of Thurlow's killing well. The night wore on. McDonald left the man alone (thinking he was Thomas, not Alfred) and went about his business. The murder would remain unsolved…for now.

On Monday, June 20, 1905, thirteen years after Thurlow's murder, Carroll was finally, accidentally, arrested. The sheriff mistook him for Charles Lennox, a killer who had escaped from jail in Butte, Montana.

Killer Alfred Carroll (pretending to be Thomas Carroll) inconspicuously ate supper with Sheriff McDonald at the Gillmore Hotel (pictured) in Deadwood. Carroll had stabbed Ed Thurlow five times at the Vincellette Ranch but was never convicted. *Closeup from LOC #2007662787, Clinton Deforest Curtis, photographer, panoramic view of Deadwood, 1902.*

But when the sheriff looked up Lennox's picture in an old newspaper, he realized he had the wrong man. Even though Carroll had, by now, grown a full moustache, the sheriff realized he was Alfred Carroll, the murderer, not Lennox.

Deadwood Sheriff Trathen hauled Carroll down to the local photographer and had his picture taken. Over twenty citizens of the Black Hills identified Carroll in a twelve-man lineup, but he stuck with his story that he was Thomas Carroll, not Alfred.

The sheriff of Silver Bow County, Montana, sent a telegram notifying Sheriff Trathen that he was sending papers to prove that the prisoner was not Alfred Carroll, as Carroll was in Laramie, Wyoming, at the time of this man's arrest.

To add to the mystery, a few days later, identification papers were received in Deadwood proving that the man in custody was neither Lennox nor Carroll! So who was he? The mystery man was released.

It is unclear if Thurlow's killer was ever apprehended—another unsolved Deadwood murder.

Killed Over a Secret

Mrs. Minnie Callison (?–1878) was one of the first women to live in the Black Hills and became the first teacher in the first school in Deadwood. She was married to John Callison, and the couple lived happily on Sherman Street. When her husband was away working in Rockerville, Minnie nervously revealed to friends that twice she'd had a terrible, premonition-type dream that a "colored man" had entered her room and killed her. Did Minnie predict her own murder?

Possibly.

At nine o'clock in the morning on August 20, 1878, Mrs. Eliza Vandaventer and Mrs. Posnansky came across a scene that would rock the community of Deadwood to its core.

Schoolteacher Minnie Callison lived on Sherman Street (pictured), where, in 1878, she was murdered because she overheard a lovers' triangle. Her killer, Martin Couk, was sentenced to life in prison in the Detroit House of Corrections and later pardoned. *Courtesy of LOC #2024692970, postcard of Sherman Street, 1909.*

Deadwood pioneer Calvin Wilson also stopped by Minnie's house that morning around eight or nine o'clock (he couldn't remember which). He noticed Minnie's window was open about two inches. When Calvin looked through the window, he saw a woman's foot, unmoving, and he said, "The woman is dead, whoever she is."[29] (It is strange that Calvin knew Minnie, had come to her house that morning for an unknown reason, saw a dead woman inside her home and still had "no idea" who the woman was.)

Minnie's body was lying in a pool of her own blood. Her head had been beaten to a pulp, and her skull was smashed, her arms bruised and her face horribly disfigured. The walls were coated with blood and brain matter. Her bedroom showed no signs of a struggle, and Minnie was lying on her back in her bed. Mrs. Eliza Vandaventer and Mrs. Posnansky were hanging around the bloody crime scene, and they commented that they "suspected" that Minnie was dead. (The "suspected" comment came up several times during the investigation and the trial, but with that much blood and brain matter, one would think it was *obvious* that Minnie was dead!)

When Sheriff Mahan arrived, multiple people had already been in and out of the crime scene area, contaminating valuable evidence. Drs. McKown and Coombs arrived around 10:30 a.m. and examined Minnie. They determined that an octagonal instrument had been used to inflict the damage, and it would have been about the size of a half dollar.* The ten massive blows to her head and body left her mutilated; Minnie's nose was completely destroyed. They believed the killer might be left-handed, due to the angles of the blows. Who would want to savagely beat Minnie in this brutal manner? And why? The crime scene displayed signs of overkill, and Minnie obviously was murdered in her sleep, because there were no signs of self-defense on her hands. She may have fallen asleep while reading her Bible, because the Good Book was still in her hands. They thought she might have been killed two days earlier. The Deadwood officers would slowly piece together the pieces of this very horrible and tragic puzzle.

Mrs. Mary V. Boughton (1841–1889, age forty-eight) lived at 498 Sherman Street in town, across the street from the courthouse, near Minnie. She ran a millinery shop in Deadwood. Although Minnie and Mary were friends, Mary played a part in her untimely demise. The Boughton family ranch was located on False Bottom, near Bell Fourche.

* Some hammers and axes had octagonal heads during that era.

Sheriffs Mahan and Brewer discovered large boot tracks, size nine, that led from Minnie's house toward Whitewood Creek. They also found a blood-soaked piece of a man's shirt below the log crossing. Mahan thought the shirt had been used to wipe the blood off an object. Could it have been used to wipe off the murder weapon?

Mr. Martin Lee Couk (also Conk and Couck, 1845–?) also lived on Sherman, next to Minnie, and he soon became a prime suspect.

Around eight thirty the night before the murder, Mary stopped by Minnie Callison's to return some dishes she had borrowed. Mary's husband, Mark, wanted to head to Rockerville, and Mary thought Minnie might want to go there with him. They all agreed. Minnie was eager to see her husband, John, who was still working out of town, in Rockerville. She had not seen him since he visited three weeks prior. (Unbeknownst to John, that was be the last time he would see his wife alive.) Mary noticed that a Professor Saunders and an unknown male were at the Callison residence.

That same evening, Mr. W.H. Taylor stopped by the Callison home and knocked on the door. He wished to grab a hand pick and some tools that John had borrowed for a mine claim he was working. He noticed that Mary and another man were in the home.

As Mary was leaving, Mr. Couk appeared at Minnie's door. He casually entered the room and sat down in a rocking chair, where he hung around chatting for about a half hour.

When Couk left Minnie's, it was about 10:30 p.m., and he headed toward a nearby saloon for a nightcap. He also noticed that General Fields, a local "colored man," was hanging around the Callison home that evening, casually leaning up against a tree. Why was Fields hanging around the crime scene?

The morning Minnie's body was found, Mrs. Vandaventer and Mrs. Posnansky were the two women witnesses at the home. They told officers that when they arrived, the front door was locked, so they went to the back of the home. When they peered in the window, they saw Minnie's bloody foot exposed. They asked a man walking by to help them get the window open, which he did. They all saw poor Minnie lying in a pool of her own blood—and they noticed that General Fields was still hanging around the home.

Others soon came forward with bits and pieces of information they thought would be helpful in solving the murder. A local named Colonel McKenna said he saw Mr. Couk leaving Minnie's house the night of the murder. He told the police that Couk passed him and that he was wearing a light jacket at the time.

Walter Couk, Martin's brother, was working at the Monte Verde Saloon the night of the murder and said his brother came into the bar at about eleven thirty and left around midnight—without his coat, seeming very nervous—and did not return.

William Terhune told the police that when he was walking past the Callisons', he also saw Couk leaving the home.

Another local, George Felix Ingram, also said he saw General Fields near the Callison home and witnessed him knocking on the front door the night before the murder. The door opened, and Fields proceeded to have a conversation with someone, but Ingram could not see who it was. Ingram went back inside his own home, which was just across the street at 410 Williams Street, and peeked out the window toward the Callison home. He didn't like to get mixed up with anything unusual.

The morning of August 20, Deputy Brewer was saddling his horse at Manning's Stable when he saw a crowd form out in front of Callison's home. He must have suspected General Fields as well, because he went to the jail and collected Fields's boots to see if they matched the footprints found leaving the Callison residence. They were a perfect match. Yet, oddly, Fields had been put in jail that very morning at ten o'clock on another charge. Mr. Beardley declared, "The hearsay gossip on the street or from old women should not be received as legal evidence!"[30]

Multiple people had seen Mrs. Boughton and Mr. Couk having drinks together in a saloon, and rumors that they were having an affair soon surfaced. The deputies learned that Couk was sharing his office with Mary Boughton and that he practically was living with her in Deadwood. Some suggested that they had plans to secretly leave town that very month, run off together and elope. But at the time of the murder, Couk's bank accounts were overdrawn, and he had made no arrangements to leave Deadwood in a safe and financially secure manner. Just a few days before the murder, Couk had paid out thousands of dollars to a mining claim he owned. There seemed to be no evidence whatsoever that Couk was planning on "running off with Mary Boughton." Couk did live next door to Minnie, so it would not be unusual for the two of them to know one another or for him to stop by for a casual social visit.

When police officers met with Mary Boughton, she seemed calm and polite but insisted that the crime could not have been committed by a White man.

When the police spoke with Mr. Martin (Mark) Van Buren Boughton (1837–1916, age seventy-nine) at the ranch, he noted sadly that he knew his wife, Mary, was in love with Mr. Couk. The morning prior to Minnie's

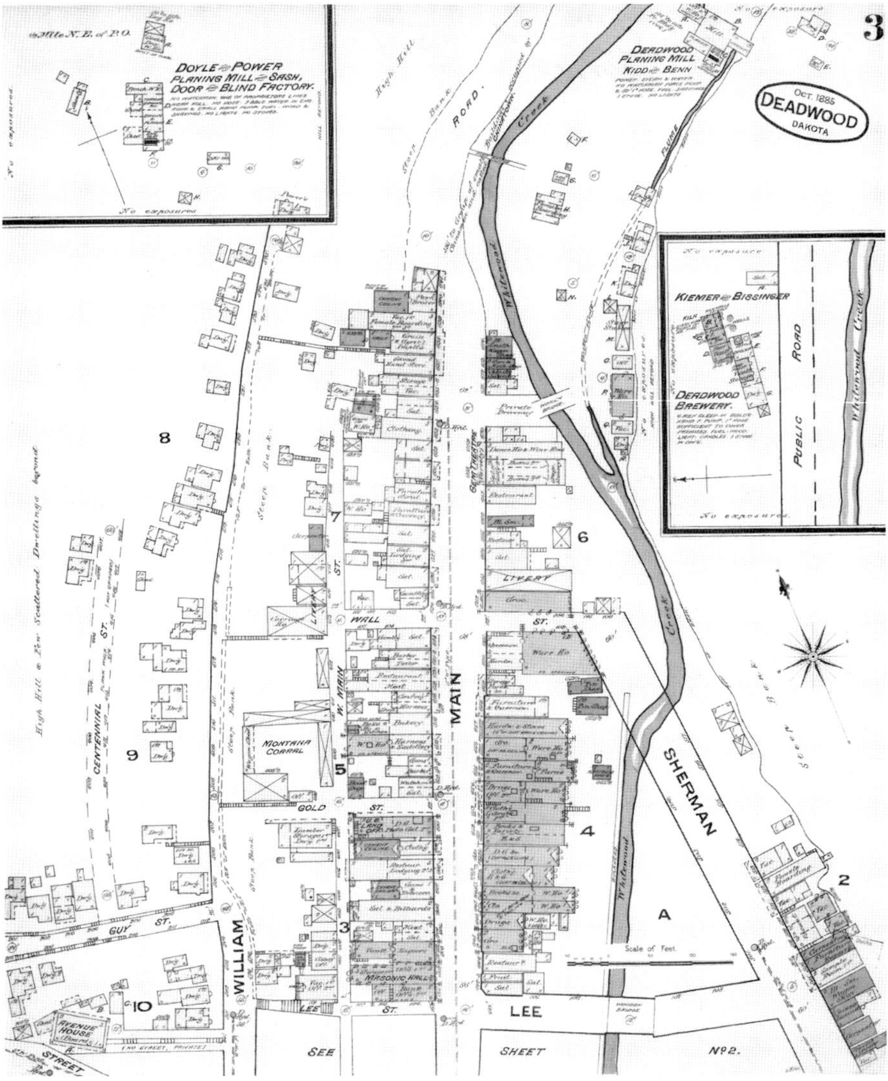

This 1885 Sanborn map shows the layout of Deadwood as rebuilt after the devastating 1879 fire that destroyed three hundred buildings and left two thousand homeless. Minnie Callison was killed one year prior to the big fire. *Courtesy of LOC# sanborn0822.*

death, he visited Minnie's house several times, wanting to know if she knew that Couk and his wife were intimate. Minnie did not answer the door. He told authorities, "I do not remember having made threats to Couk prior to the homicide. I never said I was going to kill him."[31]

Mark Boughton *was* in town on the evening of August 18. He disclosed to police that he met Mr. Couk that evening in front of the Jensen & Bliss Store on Lee Street around eight or nine o'clock in the evening. The pair went to McHugh's Saloon with Thomas for only about five minutes, and then Boughton went home. He arrived at his ranch at about eleven o'clock. Mary was home, and they both stayed home for the duration of the night. Would Couk go out drinking with Boughton if he had been receiving death threats from him? Would Mr. Boughton be out having friendly drinks with his wife's lover the night before her friend's murder? Both seem unlikely.

Mrs. Anna Simmons was interviewed, and her account complicated matters for Couk. She told the officers that Couk had stayed with her at her place the night of the murder (and he was also *her* lover) and that he sometimes roomed there. She disclosed that Couk appeared extremely nervous and unable to fall asleep, so he slipped out to have a drink. Snooping through Couk's possessions, Anna found a half-full bottle of chloroform, a bloody handkerchief and a blood-covered towel. When Couk finally came home, he went right to sleep.

In the morning, he seemed surprised that Minnie's body had been found so soon. He obviously knew about Minnie's death. According to several reports, Minnie was Couk's mistress, but if this was true, why would there also be rumors about Couk eloping with Mary? And if Minnie was his lover, what motive did he have to kill her? Perhaps Minnie found out about Mary and demanded he never see her again? Maybe a horrible argument broke out between Couk and Minnie and he had to silence her forever? But if that were true, why was there no sign of a struggle or defensive wounds? Did Couk use the chloroform to knock Minnie out and then beat her to death? Why would he use such overkill and risk getting caught?

Perhaps Mary demanded Couk never see Minnie again since she was putting everything on the line with the plot to murder her husband so they could elope together. Maybe she demanded he kill Minnie out of jealousy? Or was Mary herself the killer? Did she kill Minnie so violently because she spoiled the lovers' plans of running off together?

There were a lot more questions than answers in this case. Unfortunately, the only person who knew the real truth about who the killer was—*was the killer themselves.*

Couk and Mary were both arrested in conjunction with the brutal murder of Minnie Callison. Supposedly, Mary had a hefty $20,000 bail hanging over her head. It surfaced that Couk may have killed Minnie to keep her mouth shut about the affair he and Mary were having, but the evidence against him was only circumstantial. More rumors surfaced that Minnie was killed because she overheard Mary and Couk plotting to kill Mary's husband and make off with his property and money—a more likely scenario. Later, the elopement theory was considered debunked by many, as Mary herself provided the funding for Minnie's funeral. Or was this generous gesture made out of guilt?

Soon after the funeral, Mary began to feel ill and suffered from several ailments. She was put in jail for three days (with a new $10,000 bail, which her husband and friends put forth for her release), tried and charged with complicity in the murder of Minnie. On February 12, 1880, the twelve jurors deliberated for just one hour before rendering a verdict of not guilty and deciding that Mary could never be tried again for the same crime.

On April 4, 1880, Martin's brother Walter Couk came to Deadwood from Lead by coach. He went to the Boughton ranch and got into a fight with Mr. Mark Boughton. After their tussle, Walter filed a complaint against Mark, charging him with "assault with a deadly weapon with the intent to kill." The cause and outcome of that confrontation are unclear, as it seems to have dropped from the books.

Shortly after the end of the never-ending trials in Deadwood in the hopes of solving the Minnie murder case, the Boughtons began selling off some of their properties, obviously wanting to put the whole torrid affair behind them. Mary ran ads in the local newspaper offering lot 55½, block 6 on Main Street, adjacent to the Adams Brothers Store, and lot 43, block 6, Main Street for sale "for dirt cheap."

In 1883, Mary put the Belle Fourche ranch up for sale, as living separately from her husband on fifty acres would have been rough. In 1884, she decided to head to Livingston, Montana, to be with her husband. The following year, another Boughton Belle Fourche property would go up for sale: two hundred acres, again dirt cheap.

Four years later, in 1889, Mary died in the Sturgis Hotel in Sturgis, South Dakota. Did she ever even go to Montana?

Couk was eventually convicted and sentenced to be hanged for Minnie's murder on April 16, 1880. The execution was delayed until July 2, and then his sentence was reduced to life in prison at the house of corrections in Detroit, Michigan.

Later, Couk was pardoned, due to him knowing very influential people, and he returned to Deadwood to clear his name. He partnered with Captain Willard (Deadwood's deputy sheriff at the time) and they both spent time

Martin Couk was jailed in the Detroit House of Corrections for killing Minnie Callison but later pardoned and went on to live a normal life. Minnie is buried in Mount Moriah Cemetery, section 3, lot 83. *Courtesy of Robert N. Dennis collection, public domain, 1880, Wikimedia.*

and money trying to find Minnie's real killer. After neither of them was able to shed light on who the real killer was, Couk got discouraged.

Records conflict, but it is reported that Couk left Deadwood and lived with his mother on a farm for a year and then moved to Denver.

Oddly, he later finally confessed to killing Minnie Callison while in Deadwood and even bragged about killing several other people as well. Couk claimed that he did not regret any of his murders, except the one in Deadwood. Why? And if he really did confess, why was he never brought back to trial? Or was the story about him confessing just a false rumor, too?

In 1889, records show Martin Lee Couk was living at 1629 Sixteenth Street in Denver and was partners with John Shearer of the City Hotel, located at 1535 Fifteenth Street in downtown Denver. In 1891, he was listed as the proprietor of the Merchant's Hotel, also in Denver, located at 1723 Blake Street.

Did he go on to live a normal, productive life while Minnie's life was cut short for innocently overhearing about his torrid love life? This was possibly one of the saddest and worst cases in Deadwood's history.

What was the true story behind Minnie's horrific murder? Sadly, no one really knows.

Mistaken Identity and the Death of Bummer Dan

Another case of mistaken identity that turned into murder…

On a hot summer night, patrons were enjoying libations at the Bella Union Saloon. The first piano that ever graced the Black Hills was located in the Bella Union, so music was playing, people were dancing and cavorting—a good time was had by all! But not for long. On September 14, 1878, a man known locally as Bummer Dan (whose real name was Meyer Baum) would be dead before the night was over.

Charlie Young was known for always wearing a certain jacket. He worked as a bartender at both Lewis & Mann's Saloon on Main Street and the Bella Union Saloon. Laughing Sam (whose real name was Samuel Hartman and who was known to carry a lot of guns) was in love with an unknown prostitute who hung out at the Bella Union—the same soiled dove Charlie Young claimed to love. All three men—Bummer Dan, Charlie Young and Laughing Sam—hung out together and had a good relationship. Or so people thought.

But this particular night, something must have fueled Young's jealousy over the woman, which overruled any friendship the pair shared.

Bummer Dan and Laughing Sam were out on a drinking binge, walking the streets of Deadwood and bouncing around the bars. The two were joking around and teasing each other about who was going to buy the next round of drinks. For some unknown reason, Bummer Dan decided to put on Laughing Sam's jacket—perhaps Sam gave it to Dan in exchange for buying whiskey? The two men walked into the Bella Union, where Young saw the distinctive jacket, immediately pulled a gun and fired a shot.

Little did Young know that the man he'd been fighting with, Laughing Sam, was not wearing his own jacket—his friend Bummer Dan was. Young never got over the horrible mistake he had made. He later committed suicide in New York.

Midnight Murder in Deadwood

On May 9, 1909, an innocent man was murdered in cold blood at the home of Jennie Venable on Cocaine Hill in Deadwood.

Jennie was peacefully ironing her clothes and chatting with a friend named George Norman, who lodged at her boardinghouse. A little after midnight, there came a knock on Jennie's door. When she answered, an African American man named Ralph Walker was standing in the doorway. He had a message to deliver for Jennie. She allowed Walker to enter her home. Two Italian men, Jim Ferro and Joe Vigna, were hot on Walker's heels. Both Italians also entered Jennie's home. She had known them both for over a year, and at times, they had boarded in her home. In fact, they had also just had supper with Jennie earlier that evening.

Walker noticed that Jennie had a graphophone (an early version of a record player) in her living room and began playing some music. This irritated Ferro, and he demanded that Walker quit it. Walker had some whiskey, and the men all took a long pull from the bottle.

Ferro and Vigna moved out into the street and started whooping and hollering. Walker and Jennie told them to get back inside so as not to disturb the neighbors, but they refused.

Walker then moved back into the kitchen, where Jennie went back to her ironing, and he showed Norman his new knife. After the men admired the blade, Walker decided it was time to go home, so he got his coat and set off on his way. But the Italians had other plans.

Ferro yelled at Walker to come down to where they were waiting. But Walker was not looking for any trouble. He just came into town to give Jennie a message. Walker got scared and moved back into the house. Ferro and Vigna followed him. An argument followed, and Ferro pulled out a gun. Within seconds, he pointed the pistol at Walker's face and fired. The bullet entered Walker's skull right above his left eye, killing him instantly.

Jennie screamed, and Ferro pointed the gun at her and fired. Luckily, the bullet only grazed her cheek. George Norman froze in his boots. Ferro fired a third shot, but it went wild.

Ferro and Vigna ran out into the street and took off on the run. Norman ran to the sheriff's office to tell them of the murder, but the fugitives were nowhere in sight.

Later, Sheriff Stewart found the criminals hiding in a railroad culvert. Ferro's gun had three bullets missing from it. Ferro claimed he was living with Jennie and Walker made him jealous. He also claimed he killed the man in self-defense because Walker was bigger and had a knife.

Ferro and Vigna were thrown in jail, their fates left to a jury. After all was said and done, the jury found Ferro guilty of manslaughter in the first degree and sentenced him to fifteen years in Sioux Falls State Penitentiary, where he slaved away in the twine department. Vigna got ten years for aiding and abetting Ferro, and he spent them working in the shirt-making department of the state prison.

Walker was born and raised in Deadwood, but until recently, he'd been gone for over thirteen years. He had just got a job as a porter at Lerch & Jones' Barber Shop, and he had only been back to town for three weeks before he was killed. George Norman later got arrested himself and was charged with larceny for stealing a man's raincoat and a sack of potatoes, landing him nine days behind bars.

The infamous message for Jennie that cost a man his life was never disclosed.

Double Murder and Suicide

The bright, quaint building at 652 Main Street currently offers delicious coffee, ice creams, unique gifts and much more—but it once had a dark past. In 1939, it was the site of a double murder and suicide in the apartment facing Main Street upstairs, a tragedy that rocked the small community of Deadwood.

Around nine o'clock one summer morning, while working as a clerk at the local grocery store on the lower level at 652 Main Street, Ray Minard (who was the grocery store and building owner's son), noticed his father had not come down for his usual morning coffee and newspaper. Concerned, he made his way to the upstairs apartment to see if everything was all right.

Nothing could have prepared Ray for what he would witness when he entered the apartment. Everything was definitely *not* all right. The bloody scene he witnessed would scar him forever.

Deputy Sheriff Ted Kelley and J.O. Twiford were quickly called to the scene. There, they found the bodies of Edward E. Minard, former Lawrence County sheriff, age forty-seven; his wife, Winnie (Winifred), the same age; and their daughter Mabel Louise, age fourteen—all dead.

It appeared that Edward had struck his daughter over the head with his hard rifle case and then smothered her with a pillow. He shot Winnie in the small of her back with a 12-gauge sawed-off shotgun. He then turned the gun on himself and pulled the trigger. The bullet went through his heart, killing him instantly. But why?

There were no signs of a struggle. Before flying into a murderous rage, Edward had calmly removed his watch and his clothing, and they were set aside neatly next to his cigarettes. The apartment was clean and orderly. There appeared to be no motive for the ruthless killings. Winnie's body was still warm when the police arrived, suggesting she did not die instantly and possibly could have been saved.

The victims were taken to Schulte Mortuary for further investigation. Coroner A.S. Jackson performed the autopsies and concluded that the murders took place at about four or five o'clock in the morning on August 23.

When the son, Ray, was interviewed, he said his dad had been despondent and brooding lately but he did not know why.

Edward Minard had been a well-known Deadwood resident for thirty years, since 1909. Prior to that, he had lived in Luverne, Minnesota. He had established the Arnold & Minard Grocery Store in Deadwood with his partner, and later, his son, Ray, purchased the store from them.

In May, prior to the killings, Edward signed up for a golf tournament with his son. The only slight indication of trouble dated to January, when Edward was delinquent on his personal taxes: he owed forty-five dollars, and that debt went to bill collections.

It seems unlikely that a reasonable man would kill his family and then himself over unpaid taxes. No further information could be found about why this terrible tragedy occurred. There is always more to the story, but this sad true tale takes the cake.

A WOMAN, A TEMPER AND A SIX-SHOOTER DON'T MIX!

Elizabeth Lovell came to Deadwood in 1876 from Waterman Station, Illinois, and settled in a small cabin in an area called Elizabethtown. (Elizabethtown was a small mining camp in Deadwood Gulch located at the base of the Brown Rocks, extending toward lower Main Street where Spring Creek and Whitewood Creek met.) She was a widow; her husband had been a sea captain. She opened a restaurant and lodging house in town. The lure of gold may have been what brought Elizabeth to the Black Hills, as she owned a mining claim at the rear of her property (which ultimately caused her demise).

Lovell was a loose cannon and had a laundry list of arrests—all revolving around her guns. She shot at Captain Willard once after demanding he get off her property, but the bullet grazed her own side instead. She was arrested and discharged.

Another time, she resisted arrest for some violation or other and barricaded herself inside her home with two loaded guns and a vial of poison. When officers attempted to arrest her, she threatened that if they tried to come into her house, she would shoot at them and then drink the poison. The officers felt it was best to just leave her alone and left her property.

Next she got into an argument with Francis Johnson over a property line dispute, which ended in him shooting at her (but hitting only the door and a window) and her shooting back at him, the bullet hitting his hand. She was arrested but let go free because she was acting in self-defense.

On October 12, 1878, she was arrested again for making life-threatening remarks to John Rogers. She got hauled off to jail but was released by Judge Barker with a $250 bail bond over her head. She and Rogers had been fighting over a property line dispute, an encroaching fence and a mine shaft being partially filled in by dirt at her claim.

On the fatal night, Rogers was peacefully eating dinner at his home when Elizabeth came rushing into his living room. She shoved her six-shooter at Rogers and pulled the trigger. Luckily, she missed him.

Irritated, Elizabeth turned and began marching back to her home. Rogers quickly grabbed his nearby gun and aimed it at his assailant. He pulled the trigger five times.

Mr. Murtch, Lovell's helper (and rumored lover) came running to the bloody scene. He picked up her soon-to-be-corpse and began carrying her back to her house. Dr. McKown was called to help Elizabeth, but there was nothing he could do for her. She died just thirty minutes after the shootout.

The frazzled Rogers moved toward his couch and sat down. Dr. Dickinson came quickly to his aid. Later, he was tried and acquitted on all charges, as the jury felt he was clearly acting in self-defense. Rogers was well-liked in Deadwood and was the manager at the Metropolitan Theater. His wife was an actress at Langrishe's Theater in town.

All of Elizabeth's personal belongings went into probate court, organized by S.T. Butler. An auction was held at a jewelry store on Main Street, where a gold watch, three diamond rings, a gold chain and a cooking stove all were on display for bids.

No one attended Elizabeth Lovell's funeral. No one shed a single tear over her passing—except possibly Mr. Murtch.

The Murder of California Joe

I have traveled a good many years, having seen much of the world, but have now determined to settle down in the [Black] *Hills, and make them my home.*
—California Joe, quoted in the Bismark Weekly Tribune, *January 26, 1876*

One of Wild Bill Hickok's good friends was California Joe (also Joseph Milmer, Meiner and Hawkins; his real name was Moses Embree Milner, 1829–1876, age forty-seven). In 1864, he acquired his lifelong nickname, California Joe. He introduced himself to miners simply as Joe, and when they asked where he came from, he said California. His new nickname just stuck.

California Joe first visited California in 1849, where he was introduced to the mining industry; he'd been hooked ever since. He actively followed all the Western Stampedes—such as the California Gold Rush (1848–55) and the Black Hills Gold Rush (1874–77)—throughout the United States, but he always said that of all the places he'd traveled, he loved the Black Hills the best. Some suggest he traveled with General Custer in Arizona and Colorado as a well-known scout for the man and also worked as a guide for General Dodge. He spent twenty long years living on the plains and was a well-trusted guide to everyone.

In the summer of 1875, when gold was discovered in French Creek (an intermittent stream located in the Black Hills, running through Custer State Park), 500 miners flooded the Black Hills searching for their own fortunes. By January 1876, that number had increased to 1,200 men, coming to the Black Hills at the rapid rate of 50 to 70 per day. Rations were kept plentiful for the men: bacon cost 25 cents, coffee 50 cents and tobacco $1.60.

While tenderfeet and inexperienced men are constantly leaving the Black Hills, all practical miners are satisfied with the mines—not one has left. Indeed, this is the general testimony of all who have come in from the Hills, and it proves but one thing, that there is wealth in the country, and they believe it to be within their grasp. This ain't no poor man's diggings, this ain't.
—California Joe, April 5, 1876[32]

California Joe began running wagon trains from Bismarck, North Dakota, to the Black Hills, specifically the Deadwood mines. In April 1876, during the gold rush period, he helped guide two to three hundred eager men the long and dusty 176 miles, which took ten days to complete.

Left: Wild Bill Hickok once said, "I only have two trusty friends: one is my six-shooter, and the other is California Joe." Pictured is California Joe in 1874. *Courtesy of David Francis Barry, photographer, public domain, via Wikimedia Commons.*

Below: Wagon teams carrying supplies were often pulled by strong oxen like these, pictured in 1889. California Joe ran wagons from Bismarck, North Dakota, to Deadwood; the trip was 176 miles and took ten days. *Courtesy of LOC #99613950, John C.H. Grabill, photographer, 1889.*

In May 1876, some claimed that California Joe, alongside John Wallace "Captain Jack" Crawford (1847–1917, age sixty-nine) and a group of men, ambushed some twenty-three Lakota warriors, killing fifteen of them.

California Joe was well known for hanging out with all the big names: Wild Bill Hickok, Buffalo Bill, Texas Bob Heckle and Colorado Charlie. And he always wore his signature black hat. "I only have two trusty friends: one is my six-shooter, and the other is California Joe," Wild Bill Hickok once said.[33]

When his best friend, Wild Bill Hickock, was murdered, California Joe was in complete shock. After the ridiculous trial that set the killer, Jack McCall, free to go, rumors started that California Joe had hunted McCall down while he was panning for gold in Whitewood Gulch. Joe marched down to the riverbank and motioned the man he wished to kill to come closer. He then proceeded to vent his anger at McCall and told him to get out of the county immediately. He also promised that if McCall refused, one of them would soon be six feet underground.

On cue, McCall quickly left the area. (He later turned up in Yankton, South Dakota, where he was again arrested because he was caught bragging about killing Wild Bill Hickok.)

On October 29, 1876, the leaves were starting to turn golden hues, and everyone was getting prepared for winter. The quiet beauty would soon be shattered, and a man would be dead.

A man named George (also Tom) Newcomb was working late in the butcher shop at Camp Robinson (now Fort Robinson). California Joe and Newcomb had a slight fight over a little misunderstanding. After a few heated words, California Joe suggested they settle their dispute like men—over a few shots of whiskey. (California Joe had an extreme love for booze.) Innocently, California Joe turned to head over to the bar, thinking Newcomb would simply follow and they'd have a friendly drink together. But that was not the case.

As soon as Joe turned his back, Newcomb fire a shot that raged through California Joe's body, killing him instantly. Everyone in the saloon froze—stunned at the sight, afraid to move a muscle.

Newcomb was promptly arrested and put in jail by Sheriff Seth Bullock in Deadwood, to be tried for the senseless murder of the well-traveled and well-liked California Joe.

In his defense, Newcomb blamed California Joe for the murder of a man named John Richard (one of General Crook's scouts) during the Big Horn expedition. Unfortunately, Newcomb was tried in haste, quickly dismissed and released back into the world. He was never seen again. (Later, it would be revealed that California Joe was not anywhere near the Richards' farm at the time of John's murder and that the Sioux Indians were actually responsible for the killing.)

California Joe was buried with full military honors due to his incredible service as a scout during his lifetime. His final resting place is at Fort McPherson National Cemetery in Maxwell, Lincoln County, Nebraska. (He was originally buried in the Fort Robinson Cemetery, but later, his remains were moved to the Fort McPherson National Cemetery.)

His original grave marker read:

> *California Joe is entitled to live in history as one of the most noted scouts of the West. He was not the braggart type, but rather was always quiet and unassuming, making little of his achievements. Of a kind disposition, he had few enemies. A quick temper was his greatest fault but when wrong he was always ready to admit it. He was known as one of the strongest men on the frontier. With nerves of steel and the strength of a lion, he never knew the meaning of fear.*

Deadwood's personal connection—and forever gratefulness—to California Joe is that he was responsible for scaring the daylights out of Wild Bill Hickok's killer, Jack McCall, while McCall was panning for gold on the riverbank at Whitewood Gulch. California Joe was a true friend to Wild Bill Hickok.

The Unsolved Murder of Preacher Smith

Reverend Henry Weston Smith (1828–1876, age forty-nine), was a preacher known for his loyal missionary work and unyielding dedication to spreading the Gospel. He mysteriously met a tragic, bloody end on August 20, 1876, near Deadwood.

Smith had only been in Deadwood for three months before his horrific demise.

The morning of his murder, he left town to travel to nearby mining camps to deliver a sermon he had prepared, a journey he often undertook alone and unafraid. He pinned a note to his cabin simply stating that he was going to Crook City and that he would be back by 2:00 p.m.

But later that day, his lifeless body was discovered on the road leading to Crook City, just about four miles outside Deadwood. He had suffered a gunshot wound to the chest, but since there were no witnesses to the crime, the motive for his murder remained unclear. In his pocket was the bloodstained sermon he had prepared. In his Bible was found a letter he had written to his wife.

Some speculated it was a robbery gone wrong, but nothing of value appeared to have been stolen from Smith. Others believed his outspoken preaching might have angered someone in the lawless mining town of Deadwood, where tensions often ran high, and that Reverend Smith's efforts to bring morality to the Wild West might have angered someone in the community. His Christian mission clashed with the lifestyles of many residents in Deadwood, which was well known for its gambling, saloons, prostitution and general lawlessness. Perhaps some proprietor felt threatened by Smith's determination to bring more religion to the town, thus threatening their financial livelihood?

Or was it just an act of random violence? Given the often violent nature of the region during that time, it's possible Reverend Smith was simply a victim of random violence by a passing outlaw, a drifter or a hostile Indian.

No suspects were officially identified in the mysterious murder of Reverend Henry Weston Smith. The lack of witnesses and tangible evidence hindered any formal investigation, and the crime remains unsolved to this day.

Smith's body was exhumed in 1881 from the Ingleside Cemetery in Deadwood and moved to Mount Moriah, where he was given a proper Christian burial.

Despite investigations, no one was ever charged with his murder, leaving the case forever shrouded in mystery. Reverend Smith's death serves as a somber reminder of the dangers faced by those trying to bring morality and order to the Wild West.

DEAD MAN'S HAND

I see the game is crooked, but I'll play it just the same.
—Wild Bill Hickok

Wild Bill Hickok: legend, gunfighter, lawman, avid gambler, a true Western icon and a handsome face now seen everywhere in downtown Deadwood. No book about Deadwood would be complete without including the murder of Wild Bill.

Wild Bill Hickok, the American frontiersman, was born James Butler Hickok (1837–1876, age thirty-nine) on May 27, 1837, in Troy Grove,

Left: Drawing created from a photograph taken in 1873 when Wild Bill was living in Springfield, Missouri. *Courtesy of* St. Louis Post-Dispatch, *St. Louis, Missouri, May 12, 1895.*

Right: Wild Bill Hickok photographed in 1860, when he was about twenty-three years old. He was born in 1837 and rode into Deadwood in 1876, the year he was killed. *Courtesy of Wikimedia, public domain, 1860.*

Illinois. Before becoming a famous gunslinger, Hickok was a bodyguard for politician General James Henry Lane, also a Kansas senator. Lane was a well-known leader of the antislavery militia known as the Jayhawkers. Hickok met Buffalo Bill Cody when Cody was just a messenger boy, and the two quickly became friends for life. In 1859, Hickok was working as a stagecoach driver, where he possibly perfected his shooting skills to protect his passengers and loads from robbers. Around 1863, he enlisted as a Union scout for the Second Colorado, and he served as a spy for the Union army during the Civil War (1861–65).

In 1876, Hickok rode his horse into town when the population of Deadwood was at its highest—a whopping five to seven thousand people! (Some claim that the population was much higher.) Although Hickok was only around for a couple weeks, his untimely and ruthless murder left an imprint on the town. Even today everywhere you go in Deadwood, Hickok's handsome face stares back at you on keychains, mugs, posters, shot glasses—everything!

Wild Bill's headstone erected by J.H. Riordan from New York in 1891 read, "Custer was lonely without him." Souvenir hunters defaced it. When Calamity Jane visited the grave, the bust's head was completely gone. *Courtesy of LOC item #99613969.*

He is now buried at Mount Moriah Cemetery, right next to Calamity Jane (as was her final wish). A bullet blasted through his brain on August 2, 1876, and his legendary poker hand, the Dead Man's Hand, lives on. (Two pairs of cards, aces and eights—the final card remains a mystery.)

THE STORY OF HICKOK'S death has been told and retold countless times—but the actual facts still vary. Old Calamity's version differs from locals', which differ from reporters', which differ from his killer's (John "Jack" McCall, also Crooked Nose McCall).

The event is so ingrained into Deadwood history that even today, the reenactment of his murder plays out weekly on the paved streets and in Saloon No. 10, with local actors dressed in full Western attire, guns drawn.

It was rumored that Hickok had a premonition of his own demise. One week before his murder, Hickok told a friend, "I feel that my days are numbered. My sun is sinking fast. I know I shall be killed over here.

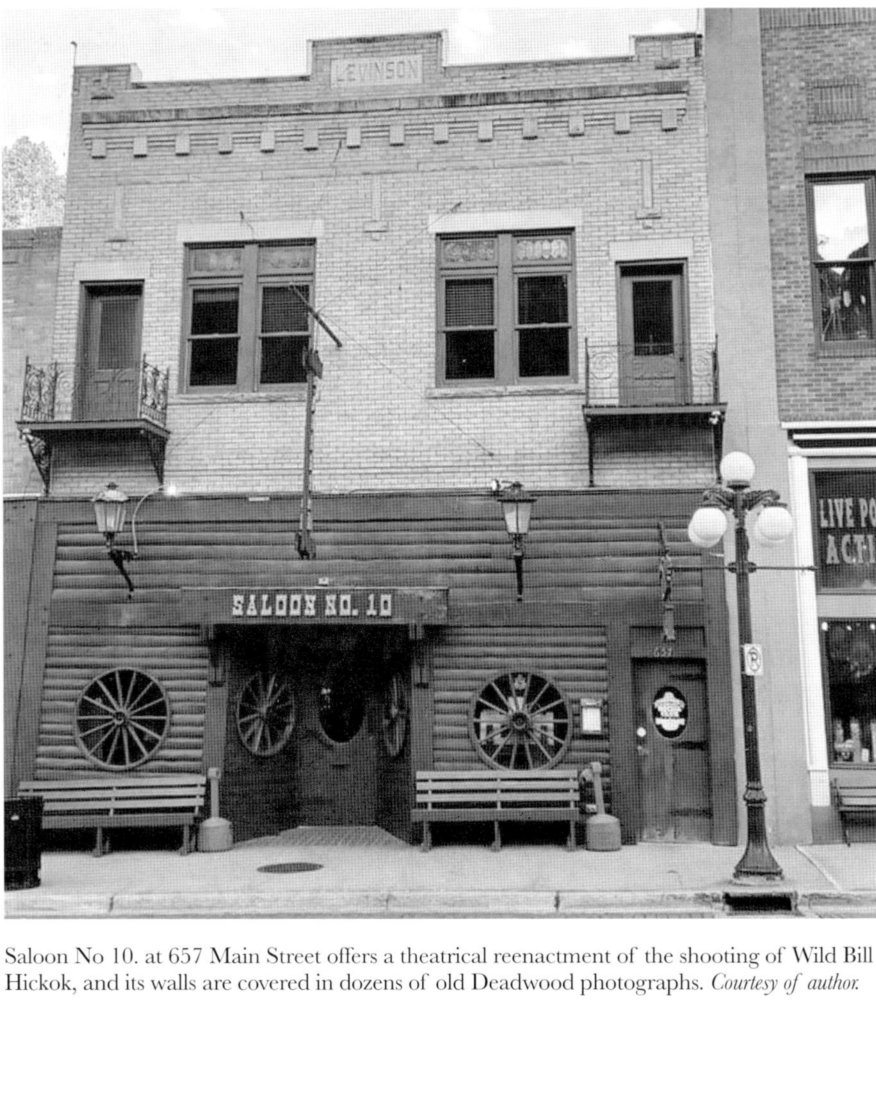

Saloon No 10. at 657 Main Street offers a theatrical reenactment of the shooting of Wild Bill Hickok, and its walls are covered in dozens of old Deadwood photographs. *Courtesy of author.*

Something tells me I shall never leave the Black Hills alive. But I don't know who it is or how he is going to do it. I have killed many men in my day, but I never killed a man yet unless it was kill or be killed. I have two trusty friends: one is my six-shooter, and the other is California Joe."[34]

His good friend California Joe (see page 89) would also be killed just a few months later in a similar manner by George (sometimes Tom) Newcomb on the Red Cloud Agency. Fort Robinson was located near the Red Cloud Agency in northwest Nebraska. The agency, established in 1871, served as an administrative hub for the Oglala Lakota Sioux, led by Chief Red Cloud, and was intended to distribute supplies as part of the 1868 Treaty of Fort Laramie. Newcomb was tossed in jail but later released.

Hickok had pulled into Deadwood in late July, traveling from Cheyenne, Wyoming, with a small group of people including his longtime pal of fifteen years, Charlie Utter (also called Colorado Charlie); wild woman Calamity Jane; and a handful of pretty young hopefuls (thinking they were getting hired for office jobs).

On the night of his gruesome demise, Wild Bill was playing his favorite game at Nuttal & Mann's Saloon No. 10.* Hickok was casually playing poker with Captain Massie (also Massey, a Missouri river pilot), Charles Rich, Frank Richards (locals called him Kittlebelly) and Carl Mann (one of the proprietors of the saloon).

Wild Bill typically never had his back toward the door, but this *one* time, he made an exception. Perhaps Bill was lost in thoughts of his beautiful new bride, Agnes Thatcher Lake, eleven years his senior, who was back home waiting for him. (They had married on March 5, 1876, in Abilene, Texas.)

Maybe he did in fact foresee his upcoming demise, as he wrote one last love letter to Agnes:

Agnes, darling, if such should we never meet again, while firing my last shot I will gently breathe the name of my wife, Agnes, and with a kind wish even for my enemies, I will take the plunge and try to swim to the other shore.

Wild Bill claimed to be somewhat clairvoyant, especially when dangers were present. He gave his many narrow escapes as evidence of the reality of this

* It's also sometimes called Saloon No. 10 and/or Lewis & Mann or Carl Mann's Saloon No. 10; records vary. The *exact* spot where Wild Bill died may be beneath a sidewalk or a building now, as so much has changed over the years.

spiritual insight. During all his fights, he claimed he was surrounded by spirits who kept him cool and collected whilst they made fools of his enemies. He gave credit to their presence for the nerve and fearlessness he displayed.

So why did his spirits not protect him during his final day? Wild Bill believed that he was predestined to be killed and would die with his boots on. He often was heard brooding over his forthcoming demise, which would put him into a deep depression at times.

The night before his murder, Jack McCall was playing cards with Wild Bill, and he felt that Hickok cheated him out of three dollars. Wild Bill Hickok pointed his trusty gun at McCall and casually told him to get the hell outta there and stay out of poker games that were beyond his tin-horn means. McCall begged Hickok for one dollar back so he could eat dinner. To this, Bill scoffed. He didn't generally win a man's money and then give it back to him. But Wild Bill gave him the dollar anyway. Instead of being grateful for Wild Bill's generosity, McCall was offended and stormed out of the saloon.

The next day, McCall was at the Gem Saloon drinking when in sauntered a stranger from outside and remarked that Wild Bill Hickok was across the street playing poker. This must have triggered McCall into thinking that this was a good chance as any to carry out his evil plan.

McCall then bumped into Frank "Kittlebelly" Richards in the street. "Let's grab a drink," McCall said to Richards, prompting him to join him at the saloon where he knew Wild Bill was hanging out. "They have better whiskey in No. 10."[35]

The duo made their way across the muddy street and casually strolled into the No. 10 saloon, where each partook in a shot of cheap whiskey. Richards saw a game of poker going on and wanted to join in on the fun. He asked to sit by Wild Bill (there was finally a free seat at the table), who nodded, and he sat down and collected some cards. The group continued the game. Richards was clueless about what McCall's *real* intentions were for going into No. 10. (One wonders why Bill did not take the opportunity of an open chair to move his seat for a better view of the door, possibly saving his life.)

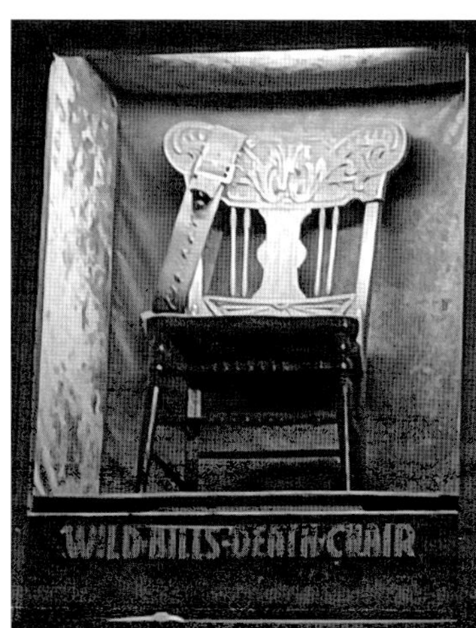

Soon, the furious Jack McCall marched right up behind Wild Bill and pointed his

Opposite: Wild Bill Hickok's "death chair" is displayed at Saloon No. 10, along with tons of other interesting memorabilia and photographs. There is a restaurant upstairs and a full bar for refreshments. *Courtesy of author.*

Above: The original Nuttal & Mann's Saloon No. 10 location where Bill was shot. It is now the Wild Bill Bar, located at 624 Main Street. The old building burned down in 1879. *Courtesy of author.*

gun directly at the back of Hickok's head, yelling, "Damn you, take that!" and pulled the trigger.[36] In less than the time it takes to sneeze, the legendary Wild Bill Hickok was shot dead.

On Wednesday, August 2, 1876, the life of Wild Bill Hickok came to an instantaneous end, at about three o'clock in the afternoon, his body quickly bleeding out on the wood plank floor of Saloon No. 10.

Captain Massie was sitting opposite Hickok at the time of the murder. He was shot in the wrist by the same bullet that went through Wild Bill's head. Confused by the commotion, he exclaimed that he thought Wild Bill shot him. (Rumors say that the infamous bullet that killed Wild Bill exited Hickok's head and then lodged inside Massie's wrist, where it remained for the rest of his life and is even buried with him!)

Frantic, McCall ran out into the street, away from the gruesome crime scene he just created, eager to make his getaway. He tried to mount a horse, but the saddle was loose, so he couldn't get up into the seat, and he didn't have time to re-cinch it. Instead, he went running down the middle of the street looking for a place to hide.

McCall ended up in a building a few doors down, the Big Horn Store, where he surrendered and was quickly apprehended by Sheriff Ike Brown and Con Stapleton, a Deadwood marshal. Calamity Jane was drinking in a nearby saloon at the time of Wild Bill's murder (some records suggest she was in the same saloon as Wild Bill at the time), and she witnessed the whole scene. Later, Calamity Jane told her version of the tale, in which she grabbed a meat cleaver and chased McCall down the street with two other local men. Calamity called out profanities at the killer until she cornered McCall in the store, meat cleaver held high above her head, holding him at bay until officers arrived to arrest him.

Back at No. 10, Dr. Pierce examined Wild Bill. He announced that Bill had been shot at close range in the back of the head, the bullet entering the base of the brain, passing through in a straight line and making its exit through the right cheek between the upper and lower jawbones, loosening several of the molar teeth in its passage and carrying a portion of the cerebellum out through the wound. Death was absolutely instantaneous.

Even so, Calamity Jane exclaimed after the funeral, "It's the purtiest corpse I ever saw."[37]

Wild Bill's funeral notice simply read:

> *Died in Deadwood, Black Hills, August 2, 1876, from the effects of a pistol shot, J.B. Hickok (Wild Bill) formerly of Cheyenne, Wyoming.*

Funeral service will be held at Charlie Utter's camp, on Thursday afternoon, August 3RD, at 3 o'clock. All are respectfully invited to attend.

There would be no real trial for Hickok's murder at the time because in 1876, Deadwood was not considered a legitimate town, as there was no state or territorial government to claim its jurisdiction. Other records indicate that its citizens were basically squatting inside the boundary of an Indian reservation already established by the federal government, and thus they had no right to even be living there.

So a miner's trial was ordered. What is that, you ask? This was an impromptu judicial proceeding that was organized due to the absence of an established legal system in the area at the time. One hundred names were written on small pieces of paper and placed inside a cowboy hat. One of the ad hoc committee members was selected to draw names out of the hat, creating the group of jurors. The names drawn were J.J. Bumfs, J.H. Thompson, J.F. Cooper, K.F. Towle, L.A. Judd, L.D. Brokaw, C. Whitehead, George S. Hopkins, Alexander Travis, John E. Thompson, Ed Burke and John Mann. Charles White was appointed head foreman. Basically, a group of local men would ultimately decide the fate of murderer McCall while situated at the McDaniels/Langrishe Theater, a prominent venue on Main Street in Deadwood at the time.

The ruthless killer claimed innocence because, he said, Wild Bill had killed his brother while in Kansas: McCall shot him dead as payback for that murder. Another claim McCall made during the makeshift trial was that he was caught cheating at cards and Wild Bill threatened to kill him for it.

Trying to look respectable, McCall wore a clean blue flannel shirt, brown overalls and heavy shoes for the trial. Judge Kuykendall was at the bench.

"I knew Wild Bill down in Texas. We were friends, and I introduced him to my family. There Wild Bill abused my friendship and betrayed my sister. For *that* crime, I wanted vengeance on him," McCall said.[38] It seems as though he felt his other two excuses weren't strong enough to get him out of the murder. (They later discovered that all of McCall's stories were complete fabricated lies. During McCall's second trial in 1876 in Yankton, Dakota Territory, the prosecution was led by William Pound, with Peter C. Shannon serving as the judge. McCall was represented by defense attorneys Oliver Shannon and William Henry Harrison Beadle.)

The first witness called was Charles Rich, who was playing cards with Bill in the saloon at the time of the shooting. He saw McCall come into the saloon and shoot Bill without provocation. Next, Samuel Young was called to the stand. He had just given Bill the fifteen dollars he owed him and moved back behind the bar when he suddenly heard the commotion. He turned around just in time to see McCall shoot Wild Bill in the head.

Carl Mann also testified that he saw McCall shoot Bill in cold blood in an unfair manner.

In McCall's defense, a few people got up and suggested he was normally a calm and normal individual.

When McCall again took the stand, he walked down from the stage and into the auditorium of the theater. He looked out at the men assembled and said harshly, "Well, men, I have but a few words to say. Wild Bill killed my brother in Kansas, so I killed him. Wild Bill threatened to also kill me if I crossed his path. I am not sorry for what I have done. I would do the same thing over again."[39] McCall then turned and went back to his seat. He had smartly emphasized, again, his original story about Bill killing his brother.

One has to remember the times. During that era, it was common to uphold the Mosaic Law, according to which "where there has been a homicide, the slayer might be slain by the next of kin." Thus, since McCall claimed (falsely) that Bill had killed his brother, McCall was completely within his rights to murder Bill.

On August 3, after just two hours of deliberation (and some rumors spread of McCall promising gold dust in exchange for his freedom), the jurors announced, "We the jury find John McCall *not guilty*. Signed Chas. Whitehead, foreman."[40]

The whole town was shocked and beyond furious with the outcome of the trial. Frustrated as well, Judge Kuykendall strongly demanded of McCall, "Get out of Deadwood and stay out!"[41]

So Jack McCall was released, given a free horse, his guns and free cheese and biscuits for the trip and told to head out of the Black Hills for good. It is reported that McCall quickly headed toward Laramie City, Wyoming—but not before Wild Bill's best friend, California Joe, saw him panning for gold in the creek. Joe confronted McCall at the Botchford Claim on Whitewood Creek and told him to leave town immediately or he and Deadwood townsfolk would kill him (see "The Murder of California Joe," page 89).

Later, while in the Laramie Saloon in Wyoming Territory, McCall got drunk and began bragging about how he killed the famous Wild Bill Hickok. The more whiskey he drank, the more boasting he did about his horrific feat. This bragging about killing one of the most beloved and respectable men on the plains in cold blood in such a cowardly and unfair manner did not go over very well with a lot of people, and they felt justice should be served.

Shortly thereafter, on August 29, 1877, McCall was arrested by Deputy United States Marshal Saint Andre Durand Balcombe and United States Marshal Major O'Brien, who turned him over to United States Marshal Burdick of Dakota Territory to be tried a second time for Bill's murder. He was tossed in the slammer and found himself in a Laramie jail for the next three months. His new cellmate was none other than Jerry McCarty, who had been arrested for the murder of John Hinch in the Black Hills just the day before the Hickok killing! On November 9, McCall and McCarty tried to escape jail, but that did not work out for them. Marshal Burdick and assistant James Bennett were eagerly waiting for the pair, pistols cocked and ready to fire. (See "The First White Man Killed in the Black Hills," page 24.)

Again, McCall pled not guilty. Why not? It had worked the first time!

Next, McCall produced a new lie, claiming he was hired by a man named John Varnes to kill Wild Bill due to a dispute that had arisen between them in Denver, Colorado.

McCall's second trial (this time a true federal one) for Hickok's murder was held at the Yankton's Gurney Hotel building and began on December 1, 1876. He was appointed the legal counsel of General H.H. Beadle and Oliver Shannon for his defense. The trial lasted until 7:00 p.m. on December 6, when the jurors found him guilty of murder in the first degree and he was promptly thrown back behind bars to await his deserved punishment.

Finally, on January 3, 1877, McCall was sentenced to death by Judge F.G. Shannon, and his execution was scheduled for March 1, 1877. His lawyers tried to appeal the sentence and asked for a pardon to boot. Both were, luckily, denied. Yes, justice would finally be served for the murder of Wild Bill Hickok. McCall would be hanged from a noose at last for what he had unfairly done to poor Bill.

NOTE: The Big Horn Grocery Store, where McCall was allegedly captured, was originally built in 1876 by P.A. Gushurst. It was located to the right of Wardner & Bittinger Wholesale and Retail Grocers. In 1877, it was renamed Goldberg's Grocery when Jacob Goldberg purchased it. It is rumored that Calamity Jane still has a six-dollar tab left unpaid! Today, the remodeled building standing at 670 Main Street is the Scott Jacobs Studio and Art Gallery.

McCall's Execution

Although McCall refused religious counsel, he did allow Reverend Daxacher to stay with him to pray until Marshal Burdick read him his death warrant.

The day of his execution, a dreary drizzle of cold rain had begun over the town of Yankton. McCall was accompanied to the scaffold platform by Deputy Marshal Ash, alongside Reverend Daxacher. McCall was given a crucifix, which he kissed and then said, "Wait one moment until I pray." Next, the black hood of death was placed over him. "Draw it tighter, so that there might be no mistake," he told the hangman.[42] At 10:10 a.m. on March 1, 1877, he was dropped (crying out, "Oh my God!"), and the noose tightened under the weight of his body.

After hanging there for ten minutes, he was officially pronounced dead by Drs. D.F. Etter and J.M. Miller. His body was cut down, placed in a walnut coffin and buried in the Catholic cemetery in town. (When the cemetery was moved, his body was dug up and reburied. His final resting place is somewhere in the Sacred Heart Cemetery in an unmarked grave.) McCall's death would be classified as the first legal execution by federal officials in the Dakota Territory. McCall was just twenty-four years old. He was buried with the noose still tied around his neck.

Wild Bill Hickok's original grave, with Arapaho Joe and Bill's close friend Colorado Charlie Utter (*right*). Utter purchased the plot for Bill's grave. Bill's body was later exhumed and moved. *Public domain, courtesy of Wikimedia.*

Wild Bill Hickok in Death

Wild Bill weighed approximately 160 pounds at the time of his death. His body was washed, shaved and dressed in a black suit complimented by a white linen shirt. His arms were folded over his chest. Hickok's trusty rifle was placed beside him for all eternity. A lock of his hair was taken from him by his recent wife, Agnes Lake Hickok, before the coffin lid was screwed down for the final time. Charlie Utter had spent his own money to make sure his best friend had a proper funeral.

The coffin was covered in fine black cloth and decorated with silver ornaments. His plot was also purchased by Charlie Utter. His headstone at Boot Hill Cemetery was a big stump at the head of his body with a carved epitaph:

> A brave man, the victim of an assassin, J.B. Hickok (Wild Bill), aged 48 years, murdered by Jack McCall on August 2, 1876.*

Wild Bill's past was full of interesting stories. The following are from the *St. Louis Globe-Democrat*, August 20, 1876.

In 1863, Hickok visited one of his friends' homes, near Marysville, Kansas. The man's wife warned Bill that ten men were on their way to kill him. He replied, "Well, little woman, don't be frightened. Get behind the chimney and we'll stop 'em." The gang arrived and surrounded the house. "Is Wild Bill here?" they called out. "Yes, come get him," Bill himself answered. As two tried to enter the home, Bill shot them both, killing them instantly. The other eight men tried to dart away, but Bill stood calmly in the doorway and aimed his rifle. He killed a third man from 250 yards away. Bill always said that was "one of the best shots of my entire life!"

In 1865, Bill owned a livery stable in Springfield, Missouri. One night, he was playing poker with pals, and he found himself down thirty-five dollars to a man named Tutt. The next morning, when Tutt arrived to get his money, he decided to help himself to Hickok's watch, which was lying on a table, instead. "By midday I will walk with it across the public square!" Tutt boasted.[43] Hickok ignored him, knowing there was more to come in this situation. At noon, as promised, Tutt gallivanted around the square with

* His grave marker would be replaced several times over the upcoming years.

the watch. Hickok marched up to Tutt, and both men drew their revolvers. Hickok, of course, was the better shot. Tutt was shot through his heart, dying instantly, and Wild Bill got his watch back.

By 1867, Bill was working as a scout for Colonel Bradley at Fort Riley, where one night, he single-handedly frightened away an angry group of lynchers that was looking for trouble.

In 1868, Hickok was named sheriff of Ellis County, Kansas. A man named Sam Strawhan was mad at Bill for killing Tutt. While Bill was sitting in Dutchman's Saloon, Strawhan marched in (after breaking some of the proprietor's glasses with a few other people out on the sidewalk). "Boys, you hadn't ought to treat a poor old man [meaning the bartender] in this way," Bill said.[44] Strawhan grabbed some more glasses, threatening to break them, too. Bill calmly shot him dead with a bullet that went right through his neck. No more glasses were broken that night.

Bill Mulvey was next to be at the wrong end of Sheriff Hickok's gun, in 1876. Mulvey was a rough guy from St. Joseph, Missouri, who liked to cause trouble. One day, while getting drunk, Mulvey confronted Wild Bill. "I have lived long enough," he commented. A nearby man said, "Don't shoot him, Bill. He's only fooling."[45] But Bill never hesitated, and Mulvey was soon dead at his feet. The bullet hit him behind his right ear. The locals cheered Hickok on in joy, as they never liked Mulvey anyway.

Several soldiers from the Seventh Calvary were next to experience Wild Bill Hickok's fury. They invited Bill to partake in a few shots of whiskey in a saloon in Hays City, Kansas. While standing casually at the bar, one of the soldiers tried to knock Bill down, but before Bill even hit the floor, his pistol was drawn, and shots were fired. Unfortunately, one bullet hit an innocent man standing nearby; the other struck one of the soldiers. Hickok left and rode sixty-eight miles to Ellsworth, Kansas, and then later to Abilene, Kansas, where he was appointed town marshal. (This is the town where, Jack McCall claimed, Bill killed McCall's brother and violated his sister.)

In 1869, while in Abilene, Marshal Hickok killed Phil Cole, a cattle trader. Hickok had already arrested several of Cole's men, and Cole yelled out that he was going to kill that long-haired son of a bitch. The men gathered in a local saloon. Bill kept one eye constantly on Cole, having heard of his threat to kill him. Cole and a buddy both pulled their weapons, but they were no match for Hickok. Cole was shot square between his eyes. No more Cole.

Bill claimed to have killed almost forty men in his lifetime. He did not know the exact number for sure.

William Frederick "Buffalo Bill" Cody (1846–1917) teamed up with Wild Bill Hickok and Texas Jack to create the Buffalo Bill Combination show. They performed 141 shows between 1872 and 1873, delighting countless viewers. *Courtesy of LOC #2021670516, F.W. Glasier, photographer, 1907.*

Wild Bill was part of the Buffalo Bill Troupe, performing alongside both Buffalo Bill and Texas Jack. He was touted as the "best pistol shot in the West."

Bill's first true love was a girl from LaSalle County, Illinois, where he lived when he was young boy. Her name was Maria Baldwin, and when he was much older, he ran into her while going to church with his friend General

Phil Sheridan. Bill and Maria recognized one another, and Bill knew he would love her forever, although he soon left town.

In the *Daily Deadwood Pioneer Times*, on September 29, 1891, the Pioneer Society explained how Bill got his notorious name, Wild Bill. At the opening of the American Civil War (1861–65), Bill was guarding a Pony Express station at Rock Creek, north of Junction City, Nebraska Territory. The McCanles Gang ruthlessly attacked the station, and Bill single-handedly killed seven (other accounts claim ten) of the gang members. Later, he told his brother that when he started to fight and proceeded to kill, he just went wild. From that day on, he was called Wild Bill.

> Note: To reserve tickets to the reenactment of the trial of Jack McCall, go to https://www.deadwoodalive.com or call (800) 344-8826 to reserve tickets. The reenactment itself happens in front of and inside Saloon No. 10, located at 657 Main Street in Deadwood.

2
MAYHEM

"Well-behaved women rarely make history."
—Harvard professor Laurel Thatcher Ulrich

In the 1800s, various forms of entertainment and devious situations led many individuals down the dark path to trouble and imprisonment. Authorities would print city ordinances in the local newspapers to remind Deadwood citizens of the things they should not do. For example, according to Ordinance No. 18, disorderly houses, drunkenness, quarreling, unlawful games and fighting constituted between a five-dollar and a fifty-dollar fine for each violation. Smoking opium would procure a fine between fifty and one hundred dollars.

In 1881, Deadwood Mayor Kirk Phillips had to remind locals that drunk and disorderly persons within the city limits or in a public space, on the streets, who acted in a noisy or indecent manner would be fined between one and twenty-five dollars.

In 1895, one could be hit with an incredible $12.50 fine for using foul or obscene language on the streets.

Let's take a look at some of the crimes that could land a person in trouble.

LARCENY AND THEFT: Larceny—such as pilfering from pockets, shoplifting or swiping valuables—was a common crime. The allure of ill-gotten gains, whether a loaf of bread or a silver spoon, often led to incarceration.

In 1902, the Deadwood Gas Company connected 150 customers to its newly established service. The town installed 30 upgraded streetlights. The $35,000 gas plant provided 200,000 cubic feet of gas daily. *Courtesy of LOC #2007662787, Clinton Deforest Curtis, photographer.*

ASSAULT AND BATTERY: Often, after drinking, fists were clenched and tempers flared. Brawls erupted in taverns, alleyways and even private homes. Assaulting another person, whether with fists, clubs, gun butts or blades, could land one quickly behind iron bars.

FORGERY AND COUNTERFEITING: The art of deception thrived. Acts of duplicity like forging signatures and altering documents drew the attention of lawmen.

VAGRANCY AND PUBLIC DRUNKENNESS: The streets echoed with the footsteps of vagabonds. Those without a home, wandering aimlessly or drowning their sorrows in spirits faced arrest. Al Swearengen of Deadwood's Gem Variety Theatre himself (under his birth name, Albert Ellis) was arrested two times on vagrancy charges, just a few weeks before he wound up bleeding to death by the train tracks. He was picked up on July 30 and again on October 19, 1904, in Denver, Colorado. Maybe he should have stayed in jail! (See "Al Swearengen's Mysterious Death," page 42).

PROSTITUTION: The soiled doves in the red-light districts whispered dirty little secrets for the cost of a stiff drink. Prostitutes, gamblers and those tempted by such vices often were bound by the arms of justice. The most popular whorehouse was the Gem Variety Theatre, a well-run disorderly house and gambling hall on Main. Al Swearengen always kept some very

NOTE: Download this panoramic photograph from the Library of Congress (item no. 2007662787) into Windows Photo Viewer (or a similar program), and you can zoom in on the picture and take a "virtual walk" through the streets of downtown Deadwood in 1902!

influential men in his pockets, which kept him out of trouble more times than not.

BURGLARY AND BREAKING AND ENTERING: Burglars slipped through unlocked doors, shattered windows and rifled through homes, leaving fear and loss in their wake. Sometimes, these petty burglaries only coughed up a few dollars—not really worth going to jail for.

HORSE THEFT AND CATTLE RUSTLING: In the old days, stealing a man's horse was considered a form of manslaughter because if a man were left out on the open range without a horse or a mule, he risked death from exposure, dehydration and exhaustion.

REBELLION: Those who dared challenge authority or harbor revolutionary ideas faced imprisonment as traitors.

DEBT AND INSOLVENCY: The weight of unpaid bills pressed upon many shoulders. Debtors languished in prison, their freedom pawned for financial woes.

In 1900 (as pictured here), Theodore Roosevelt arrived in Deadwood to deliver a speech, at the invitation of his friend Seth Bullock. Roosevelt later appointed Bullock U.S. marshal for South Dakota. *Courtesy of LOC #2008678262, Detroit Photographic Company, circa 1900.*

Deadwood's Chinatown

Deadwood's Chinatown boomed during the gold rush of 1876. At one time, the town had around three hundred Chinese residents, who ran bustling businesses located in a section called Lower Deadwood. They provided many services to locals and weary travelers but had their own police and rules that were strictly followed within the tight-knit Chinatown group.

One of the finest stores that emerged in Chinatown, in 1905, was called Sing Fat & Company, and the proprietors boasted that it carried half a million dollars' worth of goods. They claimed they spoke perfect English and could cater to any buyer. The articles they carried ranged from 10 cents to $800 (which seems far-fetched, but that was what they claimed!). The floor of the restaurant section in the building was embellished with fine ebony details, and the tables were laid with fine chinaware. Even President McKinley dined at the restaurant when he visited Deadwood.

But a few buildings down, things weren't so elegant in Chinatown. A local man named Billy ran a brothel and opium den. A mysterious door led underground, where secret, tiny rooms were built to provide sex and drugs for anyone willing to partake in the debauchery. At one time, the place was called Murderer's Alley—it had become that dangerous. Among the sleazy rooms, there was also a theater deep in the depths that entertained patrons for just fifty cents each.

SUICIDE AT THE FAIRMONT HOTEL

One of the most beautiful and well-recognized hotels in Deadwood is the Fairmont Hotel at 628 Main Street. It is also notoriously haunted, and the building has even appeared on the television series *Ghost Adventures*, *Ghost Labs* and *The Dead Files*.

Built in 1898, the exquisite Mansion European Hotel and Saloon (originally called the Mansion Hotel) caused quite a stir. The hotel's proprietors, W.N. Berry and a man named Lashbaugh, boasted many unique services newly available in 1903. The in-house barbershop was equipped with a new "rotor electric neuro-vibrator" that "made you feel like new again" for a mere thirty-five cents. The bar was well stocked with the best liquors and imported Havana cigars. One could rent a room for one dollar per day and soak their troubles away in a fancy hot Turkish bath for twenty-five cents. The Mansion European Hotel and Saloon was truly the place to be.

But by 1906, the burden of high taxes was stressing out Berry and new investor P.N. Carr. They petitioned the town's finance department to please reduce their taxes for 1903–05 to $8,000. Hopefully, a little easing of the pressure on their wallets could help the Mansion stay afloat.

But 1907 would bring sadness to the hotel. A beautiful woman named Margaret (Maggie) Broadwater (known in Deadwood as Ms. Hobson, 1886–1907, age forty-one) fell desperately in love, hoping her beau could get her out of the mess her life had become. She was originally from Callaway County, Missouri, and little is known about her. Her father, George Broadwater (1857–1897, age forty), died when she was just ten or so, and her mother, Mary (1856–1902, age forty-six), died when Maggie was a teenager. Without any guidance from her parents, Maggie soon fell into destitution and possibly slipped into prostitution to support herself. When her lover began shunning her, she took to drinking heavily. She was already emotionally unstable, and the breakup didn't help.

Above: In 1907, Maggie Broadwater committed suicide by jumping out of a third-story window at the Fairmont Hotel. She was on a destructive path over a troubled love affair. She died at St. Joseph Hospital in Deadwood. *Courtesy of LOC #2011630205, Carol M. Highsmith, photographer, 1946.*

Left: The beautiful Fairmont Hotel was built in 1898 and then called the Mansion European Hotel and Saloon. Its modern luxuries, like running hot water, caused quite a stir! One could rent a room for one dollar per day. *Courtesy of author.*

Side view of the Fairmont Hotel, once called the Mansion, where the bar was always well stocked with the best liquors and the finest imported cigars. This image also portrays the height from which Maggie made her fatal leap in 1907. *Courtesy of author.*

In late August, Maggie continued her destructive drinking and decided to finally end her troubled life. She jumped out of a third-floor window in the hotel and fell forty feet to the sidewalk below. For three long days, she lingered in agony at St. Joseph Hospital in Deadwood, suffering from a ruptured kidney and liver damage as well as multiple lacerations.

Maggie died alone. There are conflicting records of her fate. Some articles claim her body was sent back home to Del Norte, Colorado. The records of Deadwood's Mount Moriah Cemetery state she was buried there in section 4, lot 35, in an unmarked grave.

In 1915, local authorities discovered and confiscated illegal gambling devices from the hotel's basement, which were publicly burned behind the courthouse to make an example for other Deadwood business owners who might desire to break the law. During Prohibition (1920–33), the hotel operated as a speakeasy, continuing its involvement in unlawful enterprises—much to the local citizens' delight!

Today, the Fairmont Hotel is being restored, serving as a casino and saloon. The restoration is considerate of retaining many of its beautiful and original architectural features, such as the pressed-tin ceiling, ornate fixtures and wainscoting. *They also offer ghost tours!*

The Fairmont Hotel continues to be a beautiful, historic icon in downtown Deadwood.

The Sam Bass Gang

Sam Bass (1851–1878, age twenty-seven) grew up on an Indiana farm and moved to Texas, where he learned bad ways. His biggest heist was robbing a Union Pacific Express stagecoach in Big Springs, Nebraska, and riding off with $60,000 in gold. Bass worked as cowboy, stable boy and railroad freighter, but he started his outlaw life in Deadwood. There, he met Joel Collins, and a gang was quickly formed. In 1876, the Bass Gang tried to rob a coach carrying $10,000 in gold just outside of town and killed the driver, Johnny Slaughter, when he would not stop his horses. Luckily, passenger Walter Iler was able to get the coach safely to Deadwood.

While Bass lived in the Black Hills, he committed at least half a dozen local stage robberies. His criminal career came to a screeching halt when a former friend betrayed him and gave him up to a Texas ranger. Shortly thereafter, Bass and his buddies decided to rob a bank in Round Rock, Texas, so they rode into town for some supplies and a bite to eat. Little did they know that a Texas posse had been trailing them for days.

In town, some of the gang members went into a small store named Koppel's to buy a few items. Town marshal Ahijah Grimes noticed that the men were wearing revolvers. (At the time, it was against the law to carry a gun in Round Rock.) Grimes calmly said, "My friend, I will have to relieve you of your six-shooter."[46]

"I'll give it to you," Sam said. He pointed the gun at Grimes and shot him.

Sargent Dick (Richard) Ware, Texas ranger agent George Herold and ten men were on the gang's tail, and as soon as they heard gunfire, a chase ensued. Ware shot one of the outlaws in the head. Bass also got shot but was able to climb up onto his horse and gallop off. For a long three miles, Bass and his horse tried to make their getaway, but ultimately Bass lost so much blood that he went unconscious and fell off his horse. As he lay dying in a pasture, he offered to give his horse to Ware. (Other records indicate Bass was taken into custody by Deputy James Milton

Tucker and died soon thereafter, but perhaps the dying in the pasture story has more drama…)

Either way, Bass died on July 21, 1878. He died with his boots on. His final words on Earth were, "Let me go… The world is bobbing around."[47]

He was buried in the Round Rock Cemetery in Round Rock, Texas. His grave (located on the west side, near the fence) is marked with a headstone, and the site is a point of interest for history enthusiasts. The inscription on his tombstone reads: "A brave man reposes in death here. Why was he not true?"

The Round Rock Cemetery is located off Sam Bass Road, whose name reflects the area's connection to his legacy.

Grimes's widow was given one of the Bass Gang's horses and $250 for her loss.

> NOTE: The phrase *died with his boots on* was popular during the Wild West era. It implied that the person died living his (or her) life to the fullest, while being active and, more than likely than not, died while looking danger right in the face!

THE CURRY GANG

One of the most famous, ruthless and aggressive gangs back in the day was called the Curry Gang. (These gang members bounced around between the Hole in the Wall Gang and the Butch Cassidy Gang, along with a few others).

The gang took to stealing cattle, slaughtering the herd themselves and selling the meat to camp workers on the railroad lines. The men were skilled at altering the brands on the cows' hides prior to butchering them, to avoid recognition from the police. They would simply add an extra

Harvey Logan, or "Kid Curry," who was called the bad apple of the Wild Bunch Gang, managed to escape from the Lawrence County Jail in Deadwood on October 31, 1897. *Courtesy of LOC #2004682432, inscribed on item back: "Harvey Logan after suicide Rifle, Col. 7/9/1904 following hold up of Denver Bank Rio Grande train #5 at Parachute, Colorado, July 7, 1904. From the records of Pinkerton's National Detective Agency."*

Pictured are examples of old branding irons, used to mark cattle and help prevent the theft and illegal sale of livestock. Unfortunately, rustlers were gifted at modifying brands to avoid detection. *Courtesy of author and the Grant County Historical Society.*

The Hole in the Wall Gang were masters at rebranding stolen cattle to alter the original brand's design. By overlapping brands, applying acid lime (to make the new brand look more weathered and aged) and adding additional symbols or letters, they could evade authorities. *Courtesy of LOC #99613914, John C.H. Grabill, photographer, 1888.*

letter or symbol to the brand. They even had a secret way to make the new brand appear aged, to better deceive.

Harvey Alexander Logan (also known as Kid Curry, 1867–1904, age thirty-seven, suicide,) rode with Butch Cassidy and the Sundance Kid. Tagging along were Walter Punteney (1870–1950, age seventy-nine) and Tom and George Dickson (also called the Jones Brothers).

These men were well known in Deadwood. After being captured for the big bank robbery in Belle Fourche, they notoriously escaped from the Deadwood jail on October 31, 1897, by overpowering jailor John Mansfield. The next day, O'Day and Punteney were captured near Spearfish and hauled back to Deadwood for their trials, but they were acquitted. Although Logan/Curry was not as well known as some of his fellow gang members, he was certainly one of the wildest. (Records vary.)

A few interesting claims about outlaw Logan/Curry:

- Killed Pike Landusky on Christmas Day in 1894
- Killed two vigilantes trailing him in Arizona in 1896
- Robbed the Clay Robinson & Company Bank in Belle Fourche (with the gang) in 1887
- Robbed a Union Pacific train in Wyoming in 1899
- Robbed a Great Northern train to the tune of $41,500 in Wagner, Montana, in July 1901
- Killed James Winters in August 1901
- Shot two officers and later escaped the prison in Knoxville, Tennessee, in 1902
- Shot and killed the sheriff in Hazen, Wyoming
- Killed Jesse Tyler in Teapot Creek, Wyoming
- Killed a sheriff in Apache, Arizona
- Killed the sheriff of Grand City, Utah, and his deputy Sam Jenkins
- Robbed a Union Pacific train in Tipton, Wyoming
- Robbed the Denver & Rio Grande train in Parachute, Colorado, in 1904
- Ran crime with Butch Cassidy and the Sundance Kid for years

Logan/Curry was eventually sentenced to 130 years behind bars. Some reports suggest he escaped and fled to the Argentine Republic, never to be seen again. Some records indicate that he reportedly died on June 9, 1904, after a shootout with a posse near Parachute, Colorado. More reliable records say he was almost captured after robbing the Denver & Rio Grande train but decided to put a bullet in his own head so as to avoid going back to prison. He is believed to be buried in an unmarked grave in Glenwood Cemetery in Glenwood Springs, Colorado.

Some aspects of Kid Curry's story—like those of many figures from the Old West—are surrounded by uncertainty and legend, including disputes about his death and burial. But one thing was certain: Kid Curry was a man you did not want to mess with!

Tom O'Day, part of the Kid Curry Gang, also escaped from the Deadwood jail by overpowering jailor John Mansfield. He was acquitted and continued his life of crime. *Courtesy of LOC #2006680241, circa 1900.*

Tom O'Day left home at an early age and quickly hooked up with the Curry Gang. Tom "Peep" O'Day (also known as Joe Chandler, 1862–1930, age sixty-eight) joined the Curry Gang when he was just fourteen years old. When it came to being an outlaw, his luck wasn't the best. He was almost immediately caught after the gang robbed the Clay Robinson & Co. Bank in Belle Fourche (he was drunk). He spent time behind bars in Deadwood but escaped after just two weeks. He was caught again while trying to steal a mule and $392. After he was released, he continued being a bad guy and went on to steal horses, landing him six years in the Wyoming State Prison. He died in 1930 in an accident.

Walter Punteney (1870–1950, age seventy-nine) had an eventful life, one full of excitement, a blend of the good with the bad. In 1888, at age eighteen, he made his way to Wyoming, where he gained the reputation of being gifted at breaking horses. He went on to run the Camp Stool Ranch in Lenore, Wyoming, on Wind River, where he enjoyed the cowboy life. He was also part of the Belle Fourche robbery and was tossed behind bars in Deadwood in 1897. He escaped with the rest of them but was caught in Spearfish. His lawyer got him off on the robbery charges, and Punteney decided he had had enough of the outlaw life. In 1907, he married Alice Walker, and they had three daughters. He eventually bought a saloon in 1926 and opened up the Hole in the Wall Bar (also called the Cowboy Bar). He died at his home in Pinedale, Wyoming, on April 19, 1950.

Sam Bass was also a member of the Curry Gang at one time.

Several well-dressed men riding the Deadwood Stagecoach in 1889, pulled by a team of six horses. Many coaches were robbed repeatedly, due to the area's long stretches of isolated trails. *Courtesy of LOC#99613882, John C.H. Grabill, photographer.*

HOMESTAKE PAY TRAIN DERAILED

In the late 1800s, train robberies were becoming quite common in the Black Hills. Outlaws could acquire a large amount of money in just a few minutes if their plans were executed properly and without flaws.

At seven o'clock in the morning on October 19, 1888, eighteen railroad cars were rolling out of Lead, South Dakota, heading for Brownsville. Aboard were engineer John Comminskey, fireman Reese Morgan and two section men, Anderson and Grunnell. The brakeman aboard was Dick Blackstone. The conductor working that day was William Remer (who was well known to always carry his handy double-barrel shotgun!).

The day started out like every other normal day. But today was payday in the small community of Brownsville, and the train had a steel grip loaded with over $12,000 (hidden in the right tender) to pay the five hundred loyal workers at the nearby Homestake Mining Company.

A Wells Fargo Express Deadwood wagon carrying $250,000 in gold bullion from the Great Homestake Mine in 1890. Five armed men are ready to shoot anyone dumb enough to try to rob the coach. *Courtesy of LOC #99613880, John C.H. Grabill, photographer.*

But as the train moved through Whitewood and headed toward Reno Gulch, Remer expertly spotted something unusual about the trestle. He tried in vain to stop the train before a tragedy occurred. But it was too late. The train slid from the tracks, and soon, rapid gunfire commenced from the direction of some thick bushes nearby. (Later, on inspection, it was found that some spikes and several fish plates had been removed. Fish plates were metal connecting plates used to bolt the ends of two rails into a continuous track.) Outlaws and train robbers were obviously at large.

"Throw up yer hands!" a stranger yelled out toward the train crew, and more bullets went flying.

One bullet came through the window, and a broken piece of glass pierced engineer Comminskey right in the face.

Remer quickly pulled the danger cord, sounding the alarm whistle, and then grabbed his trusty shotgun and began firing back. Luckily, a conductor on a nearby train in Woodville (about four miles away) heard the alarm whistle and hurriedly moved toward the direction of the trouble.

"Don't shoot, I surrender!" called out shooter John Wilson, a Rapid City horse thief, when a series of bullets started flying back his direction.[48]

Knowing they would not be successful in obtaining the loot, the failed robbers quickly fled the scene.

When the trouble was announced back in town, a posse of forty men was quickly formed. Any man who could ride a horse in Lead joined in on the manhunt. Off they rode, horses galloping, guns raised above their heads, eager to capture the criminals who planned to steal their hard-earned money.

Luckily, they were able to find, round up and securely capture the outlaws. The bandits were George Young, John Telford, Nickerson (also known as Spud Murphy), Jack Dougherty, Charles Jones and John Wilson. The men were quickly thrown in Deadwood's jail; their horses were kept at Dotson's Stables.

Stories about the men slowly leaked out, told and retold by locals. Charles Jones was from Spearfish and was not a real cowboy. He lived in Rapid City with a woman known as Big Laura. He played the fiddle and owned a claim with Box Elder.

John Wilson was full of buckshot and had to be put on morphine for the pain. He was placed in the "insane patient" room above the jail. He was a thirty-year-old Englishman from New York.

Clark was mortally wounded and died.

Two men named John Tilford and A.G. Nickerson were also involved in the plot.

George Young was a carpenter with no prior record, but his file did show he was a known troublemaker.

Jack Dougherty's rifle was found 150 yards from the horrific scene. The weapon was covered in blood.

After their capture, Sturgis locals said that prior to the incident the men all met up in Sturgis to plan the train robbery. They left Sturgis for Deadwood at about 9:50 p.m., and they all camped out for the night together.

Hans Anderson, a butcher from Lead, was on the train during the robbery. During the trial, he was called as a witness. He told the jurors, "I was next to the tender when the train was running slow and went off the track. I saw a large man come running toward us from the hill with a big revolver in his hand. He began yelling at the top of his lungs, 'Hands up! Hands up!'"[49]

After the trial, the criminals were fed supper and locked up securely for the night.

As jailor Harding made his final rounds at about ten o'clock, all men were accounted for, and everyone was ordered to behave and go to sleep. It would be a peaceful, uneventful night—or so the Deadwood jailors thought.

At seven o'clock the next morning, when Harding went to check on his prisoners, he discovered that John Wilson had escaped along with Spud Murphy, John Telford and Jack Dougherty. Dougherty's room was on the second story facing the French Hotel on Main Street. How in the world did he escape? (Versions of this escape and the men's resulting captures vary.)

It was later learned that Dougherty (some records claim this was Wilson, not Dougherty) used his handcuffs to break the padlock and then lowered himself from the window to the ground below with his jail-provided blanket. The officers found bloody tracks in the snow by the street (he had injured his foot in the fall). Dougherty had apparently met a friend at the horse stables, where he tried to steal Deputy Sheriff Smith's horse (because he didn't like his own horse!).

Earlier, Deadwood local James Baker had seen a shifty-looking man on the corner of Deadwood and Sherman Streets, bundled up in a blanket, with no shoes on his feet. He told the police that the man was about five feet, nine inches tall and 170 pounds with blond hair and blue eyes, around twenty-five or twenty-seven years old.

Deputy Sheriff Smith was riding back from Sturgis when he noticed an abandoned cabin with smoke coming from the chimney. When he dismounted his horse to check on the fire, Smith noticed a bloody blanket—the very one Dougherty used to escape from his room. He also saw bloody footprints in the snow that led to another cabin near the tollgate, about one hundred yards away.

From his horse, Smith slowly peeked into the window of the cabin. Dougherty was inside, and he calmly motioned for Smith to come in. But Smith was not so easily fooled. "Come out!" he yelled back, gun drawn.

Dougherty casually walked out of the cabin. Smith, gun pointed at his head, made him march barefoot all the way to the Sydney Stage Barn to secure a horse for himself. Together, they rode back toward Deadwood. The whole time, Smith kept his revolver pointed at the prisoner's head, just in case.

Dougherty was ordered to dismount—with no funny business—and was thrown back in jail. A group of twenty men had gathered around to witness the affair and the prisoner was tossed behind bars.

Law enforcement hoped that the gang's capture would alert others who felt the desire to rob trains that it wasn't such a good idea after all.

Note: To learn more about the Homestake Mine, located at 160 West Main Street, Lead, South Dakota, 57754, visit https://www.homestakevisitorcenter.com or call (605) 584 3110.

CAYUSE BILL AND THE HIDDEN BULLION IN DEADWOOD'S BEECHER'S BLUFF

One of the biggest gold heists in history played out on March 9, 1880, in Sidney, Nebraska. Within a single lunch hour, 480 pounds of gold was stolen from the Union Pacific Railroad Company's office (almost $14 million in today's dollars!).

Although the robbery was never solved, three very suspicious hoodlums came to light.

Suspect No. 1: Chet Allen. Allen, who was employed as the freight office key holder, went to grab lunch that fateful day. The strange part? He did not lock the vault that the gold was being held in; he only locked the front office door! Now who in the world would be solely in charge of 480 pounds of gold and not lock the vault?

Mysteriously, when Allen came back from enjoying his delightful lunch, the vault was empty.

Allen was tried in October that year but found innocent of any charges.

Suspect No. 2: Cornelius McCarty, the local sheriff of Sidney. McCarty also owned a saloon in town. In 1908, his saloon burned down, and among the ashes were two gold bars. Some rumors claimed the gold bars were fake, but why would someone keep fake gold bars hidden in their rafters? More than likely, they were part of the gold heist.

Suspect No. 3: Cayuse Bill (also known as Mr. Edwards). A few weeks after the heist, a man named Cayuse Bill meandered into Deadwood, seeking shelter for the night. He learned that Old Man Thomas would sometimes put people up for the night out of the kindness of his heart so Bill decided he was a good target when the time came.

Later, after Cayuse Bill escaped from jail, he and Old Man Thomas had met up, and Thomas offered Bill lodging for the night. As they were going to sleep, Cayuse Bill confessed to an alarming tale. "I have been in jail in Deadwood for stealing the bullion at the Sidney robbery, and I know where the bullion is hidden! The two lawyers in Deadwood cleared my name because I promised to lead them to the stolen gold, then we would all split the reward money!"[47]

Cayuse Bill described how the lawyers, eager to cash in on the deal, bought him a new suit and a fresh horse to boot. "The bullion is buried in the neighborhood of Beecher's Bluff in Deadwood," he said.[50]

Unsure whether he was telling the truth or not, Thomas just shrugged and tried to go off to sleep.

In the morning, Cayuse Bill told Old Man Thomas that he needed to run into town and return a coat to a friend named Skinner.

"Take a gun. We are out of meat. See if you can kill a deer," Thomas said.[47] He handed Cayuse Bill his gun and a few cartridges.

Cayuse Bill never returned.

Skinner never got his coat back. The two unnamed lawyers were conned. And Old Man Thomas never got his gun back, either.

The Deadwood courthouse in 1878. Murderers, robbers, prostitutes and drunks walked through the door to await their sentencing. The courthouse was destroyed in the fire of 1879, along with all records. *Courtesy of the* Black Hills News-Letter and Mining Reporter, *December 31, 1878.*

Later, in December, Cayuse Bill was caught cashing two false checks, one for nineteen dollars and the other for eight dollars. It seems odd that a man who knew where 480 pounds of gold was buried would fiddle around trying to cash a couple measly checks. But he got caught and was put in jail in Deadwood with a $500 bail bond over his head.

Cayuse Bill does seem to have disappeared from newspapers after that. Some figured he really did relocate the gold, dig it up and live happily ever after, somewhere hidden from the law. Or was the stolen bullion never retrieved, and is it now buried under someone's foundation in Deadwood, never to be seen again?

Note: Cayuse Bill, whose real name was William Thomas, died in 1894. After his recapture in 1888 and his subsequent imprisonment, he lived out his final years under various circumstances. He was said to have suffered from health issues, and it is believed that he died from pneumonia in Lead, South Dakota, at the age of around forty-two. His death marked the end of his criminal career, which had included robberies, escapes and various run-ins with the law.

Note: Beecher's Bluff was once a prominent location overlooking Deadwood that offered incredible views of the town. The bluff was named after Henry Ward Beecher (1813–1887, age seventy-four), a famous preacher. His name became associated with this scenic spot, but the exact location of Beecher's Bluff is not really known today.

The Great Fire of 1879

Deadwood had become a lively and profitable town due to the discovery of gold in the Black Hills. Large hotels, saloons, stores and restaurants were quickly built to accommodate the influx of people seeking their fortunes. Most buildings were made from wood, and everyone constantly feared the terrifying prospect of a fire. Within a matter of hours, a blaze could completely destroy a town, leaving it just a pile of smoldering ash.

At 2:30 a.m. on Thursday, September 26, 1879, Deadwood's greatest fear was realized. The fire alarm sounded, crudely waking everyone from their slumbers.

The fire started at the Empire Bakery on Sherman Street (between Lee and Deadwood Streets), where Mrs. Ellsher worked. An oil lamp was accidentally knocked over, and the flames quickly engulfed the walls of the bakery. The fire department was called, but they were no help; they had very little water to work with. Within just a few minutes, many more buildings were ablaze.

The flames moved from the bakery across the street to the Langrishe Theater, the *Pioneer News* office, the county records office and the Overland Hotel. The flames seemed unstoppable. All the buildings on the south side of Sherman Street were a total loss.

Suddenly, a huge explosion was felt, and the ground rocked under everyone's feet. The Jensen & Bliss Hardware Store had a big storage of gunpowder that exploded—*boom*! Then another hardware store that also had gunpowder stored in it, R.C. Lakes, a three-story building, exploded, too.

Just when everyone thought things could not get any worse, the wind changed its direction, and the flames started toward Chinatown. The firemen panicked and began blowing up buildings to try to save what they could of Deadwood. They purposely torched buildings along Pine Street (opposite Mack's Corral) in the hopes of controlling the fire.

Frantic residents hired drivers, who pulled wagons loaded with their personal belongings toward the top of the hill to safety (charging twenty dollars per load, of course).

Above: On September 26, 1879, Deadwood was destroyed by a fire that wiped out over three hundred buildings. The flames gobbled up the bakery, the Langrishe Theater, the *Pioneer News* building and the Overland Hotel (pictured). *Courtesy of the* Black Hills News-Letter and Mining Reporter, *December 30, 1878.*

Opposite, top: The Cheyenne & Black Hills Telegraph Company (located inside the Welch House, pictured) lost all but one set of instruments in the fire of 1879, making communication almost impossible. The fire cost $1,604,250 in losses. *Courtesy of the* Black Hills News-Letter and Mining Reporter, *December 30, 1878.*

Opposite, bottom: The Banking House of Stebbins held $225,000 in deposits when the fire of 1879 broke out. General Sturgis sent over fifty mounted soldiers from Fort Meade to guard what was left of the town. *Courtesy of the* Black Hills News-Letter and Mining Reporter, *December 30, 1878.*

The stress was extreme. Sober men began drinking. Disorderly conduct followed. Fights broke out, and black eyes blossomed. Sadly, the pilfering of stores and robbing of homes began.

The police quickly ordered all the remaining saloons to close. Signs reading "NO LOT JUMPING!" and "NO LOOTING!" were posted. No lot lines were to be changed, either! (Sometimes, in times of fires or casualties, people would post signs claiming the rights to a building or a piece of land. *Lot jumping*, in the Old West, referred to the practice of unlawfully claiming or "jumping" a piece of land, or a mining claim, that was already owned or occupied by someone else.)

The Cheyenne & Black Hills Telegraph Company (inside the Welch House) lost all but one set of instruments, making communication with the outside world exceedingly difficult. They hurried to make a makeshift office at R.D. Kelly's brick store, up on the hill.

WELCH HOUSE, DEADWOOD, D. T

BANKING HOUSE OF STEBBINS, WOOD & POST, DEADWOOD, D. T.

During the chaos, Casino Jack (also known as John King) was asleep in his room at Stone's Hotel. He was deaf and could not hear the commotion, alarms or whistles. He tragically died from smoke inhalation; his body was found two days later. His charred remains were later put to rest in Mount Moriah Cemetery.

The already dead body of Jennie Phillips was lying peacefully in its coffin at Mollie Johnson's house when the fire broke out. It was quickly loaded into a wagon right before the Johnson home caught fire and hauled down to the city creek as a safety measure.

After all was said and done, the fire had cost Deadwood $1,604,250 in losses. Almost all the county records were lost. Luckily, the bank vaults survived the flames.

The process of rebuilding Deadwood started almost immediately. The Stebbins, Post & Mund Building held $225,000 in deposits during the blaze, and its walls were still hot when they began rebuilding. The same was true of several other structures. Deadwood would not be lost for long.

After the disaster, men were paid five dollars a day to help move goods. Others were paid four dollars per day to help clean up the mess. Bricklayers were suddenly in high demand and were fetching ten dollars a day! Carpenters were paid about seven dollars a day for their labor.

To help Deadwood after the tragedy, General Sturgis sent over fifty mounted soldiers from Fort Meade to guard and protect what was left of the businesses and buildings.

Deadwood citizens eagerly banded together and rebuilt their beloved town, board by board and, better yet, brick by brick!

A STREAKER IN DEADWOOD?

The evening of March 13, 1880, was a lively one. A few dozen Deadwood citizens got an eyeful (whether they wanted to or not) as a man came running out of a house of ill repute buck naked. At nine thirty that night, near the county jail, the nude man was seen running as fast as his bare legs could take him down the muddy street. A second man (records are unclear about whether he was naked too) was hot on his heels yelling, "I'll murder you!"

The two men began to scuffle in the street, while many horrified and laughing onlookers watched the bizarre fight play out. The two men were oblivious to everyone watching them as fists (and a few other private parts) swung wildly.

After the fight was over, the winner of the brawl called to the crowd, "I knocked the stuffing out of him!"[51] Records are unclear about whether the streaker or his pursuer won the fight.

The Demi-Blondes of Deadwood

Mary Buckley (also known as Mollie Johnson, 1841–1889, age forty-eight) was born in St. Louis, Missouri (records of her birthplace vary). She started her life as a prostitute in her early teens. After a while, she no longer wanted to work as a soiled dove, so she became a madam instead—which was much more profitable and a lot less work.

Mollie rolled into Deadwood sometime in 1878, just in time to make good on the gold rush and the influx of single, horny men. She quickly opened a very active brothel that was situated on the corner of Lee and Sherman Streets. Her girls were known to all bleach their hair with peroxide in order to create the signature look of the girls working there, featuring uniformly blonde hair on all of their lovely heads.

Mollie threw elegant dance parties and fancy balls during holidays, and all were welcome to attend. She loved parties and frequently posted advertisements for them in the local newspapers. Tickets were sold for one dollar each.

Mollie soon took the fancy of a local comedian, an African American named Lew Spencer, who performed at the Bella Union Theater, and the two hastily got hitched by Reverend Norcross.

Sitting in Mollie's parlor during the fire of 1879 was the body of Josephine Willard (also known as Jennie Phillips), resting in its coffin. Panicking, Mollie made sure Jennie's body was moved before it went up in smoke. Locals said that Mollie had an extreme affection for Jennie and considered her like a daughter.

Tragically, Mollie's home perished in the fire and her business, too, to the tune of $7,000 in losses. But Mollie's demi-blondes continued to fascinate and entertain the men of the Black Hills, and Mollie continued to increase her bank account balance, although she did support many local causes.

But after amassing a good chunk of wealth, Mollie went on a downhill slide with her finances around 1880. She began actively filing lawsuits. In April, she filed a claim against Hattie Hartnell for $75, reimbursement for a lost diamond ring and wine consumed. In May, she filed a suit against an undisclosed gentleman for $150 for some unknown reason.

Mollie seemed to grow tired of both Deadwood and Lew Spencer around January 1883. She moved to New Orleans, Louisiana, to continue her profession as a madam and start her new life.

Her husband also left Deadwood, but he moved alone to Denver, Colorado, where his life quickly took a turn for the worse. He started working at the Adelphi Theater on Blake Street, but his performances were lacking in both professionalism and skill. Although still married to Mollie, he married an actress named Marie Zoe anyway. Their tumultuous relationship was very strained. He became aggressively jealous and began drinking way too much whiskey.

One night, after another weak and ill-received performance, he began consuming alcohol again and brooding over his new wife engaging in conversations with other men. He staggered slowly up to the bar, withdrew his pistol, muttered some angry words and, unexpectedly, shot his wife Marie in her side.

Marie was hurriedly scooped up and carried off to the Merchant's Hotel to await a physician's care in safety. Lew Spencer was handcuffed and hauled off to jail. He claimed the shooting was just an accident. In late November, Spencer was given a $1,000 bond, which he supplied, and he was released. After this incident, he seems to have dropped off the face of the earth or changed his name.

Mollie's life in New Orleans was very profitable. When she became ill in November 1889 and drew up her will a few days before her death, some claimed her estate was worth over $20,000! She left her money to her niece, Miss Mary Buckley of St. Louis. Apparently, her niece did not care much for Mollie's estate, as pretty much everything was auctioned off at her aunt's home, located at 40 Basin Street in New Orleans, on December 18, just a few weeks after Mollie's death. Her elegant rosewood bedroom furniture, delicate lace curtains, gilded mirrors, precious household goods and more were sold one by one. After all the people involved took their share of Mollie's estate money, it was reported that only a measly $952.45 was left in her bank account.

A simple grave marker at the Metairie Cemetery in New Orleans reads, "Mary Buckley, died November 30, 1889."

Prohibition in Deadwood

In 1890, the State of South Dakota thought it was an innovative idea to ban the sale of alcohol "by the drink." That meant people could still buy bottles

When Prohibition was instigated, Deadwood had its own ideas about how to manage the new laws: they promptly ignored or worked around them! *Courtesy of LOC #2001706109, Pouring whiskey into a sewer, 1921.*

South Dakota's "bone-dry" law, enacted in 1917, prohibited any beverage with alcohol content. Despite the statewide ban, Deadwood became known for bootlegging, speakeasies, secret bars and special gatherings. *Courtesy of LOC #89706120, Prohibition bottles and barrel of confiscated whiskey, 1921.*

of booze themselves and then go to a soft drink site and mix the alcohol with the pop served on-site. How this act was supposed to deter drinking is left to the imagination.

When true Prohibition was instigated, the citizens of Deadwood had their own idea about how to manage these new rules: they promptly ignored them! Under pressure from authorities, local saloons created secret passwords, special hideouts and other ways to deal with the situation. The Franklin Hotel even had a secret passageway used especially to sneak in booze.

THE POPULAR GEM VARIETY THEATRE

For a smashing good time and any sins one wanted to partake in, the Gem was the place to be. Al Swearengen's extremely popular Gem Variety Theatre was a long-standing, well-known saloon, brothel and gambling hall in Deadwood. The first Gem was built in April 1877 on the corner of Wall and Main Streets. Swearengen prided himself on offering the finest entertainment, everything from dancing girls to prize fights.

Al Swearengen placed many ads in local newspapers promoting his fabulous events and entertainers. *Courtesy of the* Black Hills Weekly Pioneer, *April 21, 1877.*

The building suffered some fire damage in the summer of 1879 and then completely burned down during the devastating fire that took out most of the town in the fall of the same year. But Al Swearengen was not deterred. He immediately began building a bigger and better Gem Theatre. Its doors opened in December, ready to rock and roll once again.

For twenty-two years, Al Swearengen ran the Gem and made sure it was a great location to cause havoc and create mayhem in Deadwood. Today, the Gem Steakhouse & Saloon, located at 601 Main Street, is still one of the most popular casinos, fabulous restaurants and beautiful hotels in town.

NOTE: The original location of Al Swearengen's first "Cricket Saloon" in 1876 was where the small Lucky Horse Company souvenir shop (all sales benefit rescued animals at their Shiloh Horse Rescue farm) now sits, at 621 Main Street in Deadwood. His first Gem Saloon was also erected on the same location in 1877.

SOILED DOVES, HOUSES OF ILL REPUTE AND DANCE HALL GIRLS

The oldest profession didn't escape the streets of Deadwood. In fact, until 1980, when the town suffered a raid by the federal government, brothels were still raging nightly.

But some citizens and city officials of Deadwood were eager to get rid of its lower-class citizens. In 1885, after a citywide fire, they rejected efforts to repair the street in the burnt portion of Chinatown, hoping this would hinder the opium smoking, gambling and sinful activities derived from the ladies of the night.

In the late 1890s, the sheriff had gotten enough pressure from concerned citizens. On November 21, he had his men raid the Dwyer & O'Dell Gambling House, arrest the proprietor and seize all the gambling devices. But they were a little unprepared to actually arrest the two-hundred-plus men and women inside who were eagerly partaking of these debaucheries! So the officers focused on making the greatest impact and impression: they would arrest the biggest and baddest of the bunch. Charles R. Dwyer (proprietor), G.H. Holstein, John O'Dell (proprietor), George McDonald, Fred Sessions and Fred Ehringer were enthusiastically hauled off to Justice Hall. They were threatened with a fine of $500 or one year in jail if convicted.

But as soon as the men were released, they set up the gambling tables again—by early the next morning! When they got raided a second time, they declared that they were confused by the twenty-four-hour rule imposed on them. Charles Dwyer was arrested again and fined for keeping a disorderly house.

During the height of the moral cleanup efforts all over the United States in the 1920s, Deadwood seemed oblivious to any concerns. It had never really created strong city ordinances like other cities had, and some officials did not feel any strong pressure to enforce state laws, either. Deadwood was notorious for disapproving of anything that would hamper its gambling, prostitution or booze profits. The city council customarily rejected submitted ordinances. Votes for and against disorderly houses were 5–3, and gambling came in at 6–2.

A few years later, Reverend J.M. Gurley tried in vain to get the city under control. He wanted a moral cleanup of Deadwood. He believed there to be forty or fifty "sporting" women in the city, and they needed to be stamped out!

Mrs. M.C. White also jumped on the moral cleanup detail. She was disgusted that schoolboys were smoking cigarettes in Deadwood. Minors were even being allowed into pool halls! She also felt that advertisements of women smoking cigarettes were very offensive and needed to be banned.

Mayor Howe would slowly and calmly relay to those concerned that he doubted the problems of prostitution, gambling and drinking within the city could ever truly be solved. Perhaps he personally understood that these so-called immoral vices kept the city alive and financially healthy?

The Wildest Mayhem Maker of Deadwood, Calamity Jane

"Deadwood was the place she loved the most, and her name is strongly intertwined with the early days of that city."
—W.C. Cresswell, the Lead Daily Call *editor, on Calamity Jane*

Martha Jane Canary, later called Calamity Jane (later Martha Burke, 1852–1903, age fifty-one, but records vary), was born in Princeton, Missouri. After a very rough and uncertain childhood, she shed the overwhelming responsibility of caring for her younger siblings after both her parents passed away. Martha came to Deadwood during the beginning of the gold rush era, in 1875–76, when she was about twenty-three years of age.

As Martha grew older, she could outswear, outgamble, outride, outshoot, outsmoke and outdrink almost any man. She had no problem wearing men's clothes in a daily basis (during a time when that was considered extremely inappropriate and improper for a woman), and eventually her fringed buckskin outfit became her trademark.

Much of her life remains a mystery, as her stories of her experiences were as wild as she was. Her tall tales and exaggerated untruths kept everyone entertained around the campfire or in the bunkhouse. She made a meager living by telling these stories and relaying her own personal history to crowds. The more outrageous, interesting and far-fetched her stories were, the more people wanted to listen to them!

Following Martha's travels via clippings from historical newspapers reveals quite the wandering spirit. She seemed to blaze a trail of chaos and excitement everywhere she went. During her lifetime, she traveled through Idaho, South Dakota, Montana, Wyoming, Washington, New York, Utah—and probably even more states that are not documented.

After both her parents had died, she set out on her own, and in 1861, she landed at a nearby fort, where the local soldiers "adopted" her. They paid

Calamity Jane loved Deadwood with all her heart. Knowing she was heading to the final frontier, she wanted to die in Deadwood. Unfortunately, she died in Terry instead. *Courtesy of LOC #2005688173, C.D. Arnold, photographer, Martha in Buffalo, New York, circa 1901.*

an old woman in town to take care of her, but that did not end well. The woman took the money but did little to take care of the child, who was found wandering around alone at Fort Bridger when she was about ten years old, calling herself Jennie.

It is recorded that young Jennie left a mining camp in Virginia City, Nevada, around 1862. In 1868, she was adopted by Major P.A. Gallager and his wife, who lived in South Pass City, Wyoming. The major worked as a lawyer in an area known as Miner's Delight. Jennie took the fancy of a young boy, which upset Mrs. Gallager. Jennie argued with the woman of the house about the boy and, after getting a stiff spanking from her, decided to move along. She hopped aboard the Missouri Pacific train heading toward her next adventure.

In 1870, Jane decided she wanted to join the army. Donning men's clothing, she arrived at Fort Russell in Wyoming and went to help General George Armstrong Custer. From 1872 to 1875, still pretending to be a man, she fought the Nez Perce with General Crook.

During the years 1873–1875, Jane was often seen in Cheyenne, Wyoming. Around 1876, she got work as a dispatcher for General Custer due to her extreme equestrian skills. She also helped by providing supplies, scouting and medical assistance to Custer and his troops. This is when she contracted pneumonia while swimming in the frigid Platte River at Fort Fetterman, which left her very weak. Although Jane was in the area at the time, her illness was probably the only thing that kept her from being in the middle of the massacre that killed so many soldiers and Indians (along with General George Armstrong Custer) later that year, the Battle of the Little Bighorn. (Also known as Custer's Last Stand, the Battle of the Little Bighorn took place on June 25–26, 1876, and was a significant battle between the Seventh Cavalry Regiment of the United States Army—led by Lieutenant Colonel George Armstrong Custer; over two hundred of his men also died—and a coalition of Native American tribes, including the Lakota Sioux, Northern Cheyenne and Arapaho, who were led by Sitting Bull and Crazy Horse.)

After Jane recovered, while getting drunk in Custer City, she was disgraced for public intoxication and disorderly conduct by Captain Jack Crawford (who, after her death, went on a tirade exploiting her bad reputation for some reason, publishing article after article in various newspapers claiming she was nothing but a "whore" and never did any of the things she claimed).

Jane's travels vary from newspaper to newspaper (as reported later), but around 1877, now about twenty-five years old, she hooked up with some unknown shady characters. She and a few others took to robbing stores. After one such incident, Jane fled back to Miner's Delight and proceeded to get drunk. She began bragging about their take with partners Bill Blivens and a man known as Red. Jane reportedly asked Blivens to kill Red, and when he refused, she threatened Red herself: "Leave or die!" In 1888, Blivens was arrested in Landers, Wyoming, as an escaped convict; he later died in the Wyoming Penitentiary. Red wound up in the Ohio Penitentiary. (Bill Blivens was also involved in the incredible Sidney, Nebraska heist on March 9, 1880, in which 480 pounds of gold was stolen, along with robbers Cayuse Bill, Spud Murphy and John Telford. See "Cayuse Bill and the Hidden Bullion in Deadwood's Beecher's Bluff," page 125.)

Jane married Clinton Burke in 1884 (some records indicate 1885), and they had a daughter together.

In 1885, Jane holed up somewhere in Landers, Wyoming. That year, Calamity Jane was known to have joined a traveling circus, and she eventually became part of the Wild West shows that toured around the country. She sometimes performed under the name Calamity Jane, the Woman Scout, capitalizing on her frontier persona to entertain audiences who were fascinated by the Wild West.

In 1890, she was living in Rock Springs, Wyoming. She was married to Frank Steers (sometimes spelled Streeter) and was calling herself Jane Steers. Their marriage was brief.

In the 1890s, Calamity Jane briefly performed in Buffalo Bill's Wild West Show. She would tell tall tales about her adventures, sell self-portraits and pamphlets and occasionally even sing onstage (though her talents as a real singer were very questionable). Some claims state Calamity Jane also married Clint Flatt, a man she had met while traveling with the Wild West shows. Their marriage was also short-lived.

Newspapers have her living in Omaha, Nebraska, in 1892.

Jane arrived in Deadwood from Bell Fourche in October 1895. Stagecoach driver Hank Jewett remembered her stepping off the coach with a nine-year-old girl (the age would be about right if it were her daughter by Burke). The pair went to rent a room at Wright's Boarding House on Upper Sherman Street, and Jane signed the register using the name Mrs. Burke. That day, she went and sat with Sheriff Remer for over an hour in his office, behaving herself. She explained she had been living with Burke on a ranch about fourteen miles from Ekalaka, Montana. She did not explain why she and the little girl were in Deadwood alone.

The year 1896 brought Jane a custody battle over her daughter in the courtroom (which she lost). Later, she traveled to Chicago, Illinois, to work the crowds at various expositions. Calamity was working hard as a book agent and selling her biographical pamphlet to anyone who would purchase it, to earn money to educate her daughter. She returned to Deadwood that same year and hooked up with a local man named Baker.

"Calamity Jane was always one of the boys. No devilish scheme could be concocted without her assistance, and she was always an enthusiastic part in all the rough experiences which the men of the territory enjoyed," said Dr. Hancher in 1898.[52]

It is unclear how many children Calamity Jane bore in her lifetime. She also was prone to adopting children who were left alone in the world. Although these children often did not live with her long, she always had fond memories of them.

Jane learned to manage a horse at an early age and was known to be a most talented rider. One of her favorite horses was a wild mustang that she broke and managed to ride successfully. She named the mare Sioux Sue. The mustang was part of a large herd that wandered the Badlands. Once the mare was captured and somewhat tamed, Jane was the only person who could stay on top of her. It was said that Sioux Sue had the intellect of a human and could withstand hardships that would cause a normal horse to perish and handle hard situations that would kill other horses.

The Nickname Calamity Jane

Many stories have been told about where and when she adopted the name Calamity Jane. One of the more popular ones was that she saved Captain Egan at Goose Creek (now Sheridan, Wyoming) when he was ambushed by Indians. Jane rode over to Egan, scooped him up and brought him back to the fort. When both the captain and Jane were safe, Egen looked up at her and said, "You are a good person to have around in times of calamity"—thus her new nickname.[53] Some historians have cast doubt on this theory, stating that it would have been impossible for Jane to lift the Captain from the ground and thrust him onto the back of her horse. Keep in mind that Jane was five foot three and approximately 125 pounds during her prime. It would have been very difficult for her to perform that feat. Later, in 1896, she finally told a reporter for the *Helena Independent* the real story of how she got her name:

> *It was on Goose Creek where Captain Egan was in command of the post. We were ordered to quell an uprising of the Indians, and were out for several days, had numerous skirmishes, during which six of the soldiers were killed and several wounded. When returning to the post, we were ambushed about a mile and a half from our destination. When fired upon Captain Egan was shot. I was riding in advance and on hearing the firing turned in my saddle and saw the Captain reeling in his saddle as though about to fall. I turned my horse and galloped back with all haste to his side and got there in time to catch him as he was* falling *from his saddle. I lifted him onto my horse in front of me and succeeded in getting him safely to the fort. Captain Egan on recovering laughingly said, "I name you Calamity Jane the heroine of the Plains." I have born that name up to the present time.*[54]

This story is more plausible. The average man in the 1880s was only about five foot five and weighed 150 pounds. Jane could have easily moved him from his saddle to hers as he was falling off.

J.P. Poulton, editor of the *Cheyenne Sun*, often wrote about Calamity's travels. While some papers loved to discuss Jane's drunkenness and rowdy behavior, Poulton preferred to speak kindly of her. "There was one thing about Calamity Jane: good, bad, or indifferent, she was a good nurse and took care of every sick person she could reach. If she heard of a sufferer, she would ride all day to offer her services and when she was keeping boarders in a mining camp every miner for miles around came to her for doctoring."[55]

But Calamity was certainly attracted to lawlessness. It seemed to call out to her inner core. In September 1901, she was arrested for public drunkenness and creating a disturbance. She asked Buffalo Bill for twenty-five dollars for a train ticket to get her to go to Livingston, Montana. She did not let the moss grow under her feet, ever.

Jane would suffer through numerous employment struggles, a few more marriages and many more arrests, and eventually she ended up in the poorhouse, expecting to die there. But somehow, she survived, and locals pooled their money to help her out.

Many people do not believe that Calamity actually did the things she claimed she did during her adventurous and unpredictable life. They say she was never a scout, that she never killed anybody, that she was just a drunk old prostitute. Yet in 1902, Buffalo Bill himself spoke of how Calamity Jane was appointed as a scout to General Crook—and he had no reason to lie.

No stranger to booze, Martha would drink away her last penny. She struggled with alcoholism her entire life, and in the end, the whiskey is what killed her. Her bowels were severely inflamed, and the doctors felt there was no cure for her ailment, especially if she continued to drink alcohol.

When she knew her end was drawing near, she said, "All my old Pards have gone over the Great Divide and I am ready to go, too."[56]

The legendary Calamity Jane died on August 1, 1903, in an upstairs room at the Callaway Hotel (also spelled Calloway, but the 1903 Sanborn map spells it with an *a*) in Terry, South Dakota, about eight miles from Deadwood. Her funeral was held at the Methodist church in Deadwood, and hundreds of people came to pay their respects.

Oddly, there was a rumor that mourners began snipping off parts of Jane's hair and the funeral directors had to put a wire cage over her head to discourage the morbid souvenir takers.

Calamity Jane died penniless and most likely alone, a sad ending to the story of such a fascinating and exciting woman so full of life. She never let anyone suffer, would go to great lengths to ensure the sick were cared for and always entertained whoever had the pleasure of being in her company, whether she was behaving herself or not!

CONCLUSION

This wraps up our whirlwind virtual stagecoach trip through historic Deadwood! I hope you have enjoyed learning about the old-timers, proprietors and locals who created the small town of Deadwood—one that has become a legend in its own time.

Back in 1875, when the pioneers were struggling to clear the dead wood and tree trunks from where they wanted to set up town (hauling them off with the help of strong men, oxen and horses)—in their wildest dreams, they would have never thought that their small town would become a big hit HBO series, a very popular tourist destination and an extremely profitable part of South Dakota. But it has and will continue to fascinate and entertain crowds for many years to come.

See you soon, pardner!

NOTES

1. *Yankton Press and Union and Dakotaian*, "The Hinch Murder in the Black Hills," August 24, 1876.
2. *Weekly Pioneer-Times*, "Tha Deliberately Planned the Murder," November 23, 1893.
3. *Weekly Pioneer-Times*, "Farnham Can Not Appear," March 2, 1905.
4. *Weekly Pioneer-Times*, "Tells of the Shooting," June 1, 1905.
5. *Weekly Pioneer-Times*, "Died as She Lived," Thursday, December 21, 1893.
6. Ibid.
7. Ibid.
8. *Weekly Pioneer-Times*, "The Yusta Murder Trial," Thursday, March 8, 1894.
9. *Weekly Pioneer-Times*, "Died as She Lived," December 21, 1893.
10. *Weekly Pioneer-Times*, "The Yusta Murder Trial," March 8, 1894.
11. *Oskaloosa Herald*, "Close Call for L.A. Swearengen," October 6, 1904.
12. From Coroner's Report on Albert Ellis (Swearengen), courtesy of the Denver Public Library Special Collections, item WH842, courtesy of reference librarian Alex Hernandez.
13. *Deadwood Pioneer Times*, March 12, 1880.
14. *Deadwood Daily Pioneer Times*, October 29, 1927.
15. *Black Hills Weekly Times*, "Shooting of Mr. J.C. Tuttle," September 9, 1877.
16. *Black Hills Weekly Times*, "The Homicide at Keet's Mine," September 9, 1877.
17. Find a Grave, "James Leighton Gilmore," https://www.findagrave.com; *Daily Deadwood Pioneer-Times*, "Outraged Law," December 16, 1882.

18. *Yankton Press and Dakotaian*, "Gilmore's Crime," December 19, 1882.
19. Warren Mornell, "Thru the Hills," *Rapid City Journal*, April 11, 1949.
20. *Union County Courier*, "Charles Brown Hanged," July 22, 1897.
21. *Deadwood Evening Independent*, "Dropped to Death," July 14, 1897.
22. Jerry Bryant and Bill Markley, "Death of Deadwood's China Doll," HistoryNet.com, June 20, 2017, https://www.historynet.com.
23. *Black Hills Weekly Times*, "Sudden Death," May 11, 1889.
24. Ibid.
25. Ibid.
26. *Deadwood Pioneer-Times*, "A Verdict Reached," May 11, 1889.
27. *Deadwood Pioneer-Times*, "Shocking Tragedy," April 29, 1878.
28. *Daily Deadwood Pioneer-Times*, "Stabbed to Death," March 24, 1892.
29. *Black Hills Weekly Pioneer*, "Mondays Proceedings," February 21, 1880.
30. *Daily Deadwood Pioneer-Times*, September 12, 1878.
31. Kaija Swisher, "A Silver-Tongued Murderer?" *Black Hills Pioneer*, November 16, 2018.
32. *Bismarck Weekly Tribune*, "California Joe," April 5, 1876.
33. *Morning Herald*, "Wild Bill's Presentiment," September 8, 1876.
34. Ibid.
35. *Wichita Star*, "Wild Bill's Death," July 17, 1890.
36. *Deadwood Weekly Pioneer Times*, February 28, 1880.
37. *Deadwood Pioneer-Times*, "Kansas Marshal Is Murdered in Saloon," June 8, 1876.
38. *Maitland Mercury*, "Lynch Jury's Verdicts," May 12, 1896.
39. *Deadwood Pioneer-Times*, "Early Days," February 28, 1880; *Inter Ocean*, "The Lynch Jury's Queer Verdict," November 17, 1895.
40. *Black Hills Weekly Times*, "Pioneer Days," April 13, 1889.
41. *Deadwood Pioneer-Times*, "McCall Is Innocent, Justice Miscarries," June 8, 1876.
42. *Yankton Press and Union and Dakotaian*, "The Gallows," March 8, 1877.
43. *St. Louis Post-Dispatch*, "Wild Bill's Famous Duel," May 12, 1895.
44. *Carrollton Democrat*, "Daring Deeds of the Murdered Scout," August 25, 1876.
45. *Holton Recorder*, "Wild Bill: Sam Strawhan Shot Dead," August 31, 1876.
46. Historic Round Rock Collection, "The Story of Sam Bass," https://www.roundrocktexas.gov; Bob Boze Bell, "Bad Day at Round Rock," *True West*, June 1, 2010, https://truewestmagazine.com.
47. *Galveston Daily News*, "Sam Bass and His Band," July 24, 1878.
48. *Deadwood Pioneer-Times*, "Remer's Pluck," October 13, 1888.
49. *Deadwood Pioneer-Times*, "A Tough Gang," October 20, 1888.
50. *Black Hills Weekly Pioneer*, "Bullion Racket," March 26, 1881.
51. *Daily Deadwood Pioneer-Times*, "An Exciting Affair!" March 9, 1880.

52. *Kansas City Journal*, "Calamity Jane," December 26, 1898.
53. *Tonopah Bonanza*, "Calamity Jane," August 22, 1903.
54. *Helena Independent*, "Turned Book Agent," September 24, 1896.
55. *News and Advance*, "Calamity Jane in Jail," February 10, 1903.
56. *Weekly Pioneer-Times*, "Passing of Calamity Jane," August 13, 1903.

SOURCES BY CHAPTER

INTRODUCTION

Aikman, Duncan. "Deadwood the Dreadful." *Deadwood Daily Pioneer Times*, October 28, 1927.

Brown, Jesse, and A.M. Willard. *The Black Hills Trails: A History of the Struggles of the Pioneers in the Winning of the Black Hills.* Rapid City Journal Company, 1924.

Oshes, Janet. "Mt. Moriah Cemetery Has a Colorful and Violent Past." *Black Hill Weekly Times*, April 16, 1980.

1. MURDERS IN DEADWOOD AND THE BLACK HILLS

The First White Man Killed in the Black Hills

Black Hills Weekly Pioneer, August 5, 1876.

Deadwood Pioneer-Times, March 7, 1880.

Ghastly Triple Murder at Sawpit Gulch

Daily Deadwood Pioneer-Times, November 18 and 23, 1893.

Weekly Pioneer-Times, November 23, 1893.

Murder at Queen of the Hills

Canton Farmers Leader, June 2, 1905.
Hot Springs Weekly Star, May 5, 1905.
Weekly Pioneer-Times, March 30 and June 1, 1905.

An Exploding Tire Pump and Death

Daily Deadwood Pioneer-Times, September 10, 11, 12 and 25, 1926.
Lead Daily Call, September 13, 1926.
Lincoln Journal Star, September 7, 1926.
Queen City Mail, September 15, 1926.

The Mascot Saloon and a Lovers' Triangle

Black Hills Weekly Times, December 23, 1893.
Weekly Pioneer-Times, December 21 and 28, 1893.

Henry Clark: Killed Over a Saddle?

Deadwood Pioneer-Times, February 14, 1883.
Democratic Age, February 14 and 15, 1883.
Lebanon Daily News, February 15, 1883.

Al Swearengen's Mysterious Death

Black Hills Weekly Pioneer, May 26, 1877.
Black Hills Weekly Times, July 13, 1893.
Daily Deadwood Pioneer-Times, March 13, 1892, and December 20, 1899.
Deadwood Pioneer-Times, July 7, 1881.
Des Moines Register. "Oskaloosa Man Shot in the Dark." October 2, 1904.
Hernandez, Alejandro. "Deadwood's Despicable Mack Daddy Al Swearengen: The Brothel Owner Abused 'Soiled Doves' in Dakota Before Karma Came Calling in Denver." HistoryNet.com, January 5, 2024.

Lead Daily Call, December 30, 1904.
Missouri Valley Times, July 21, 1910.
Sioux City Journal, July 15, 1910.
Weekly Pioneer Times, October 22, 1903.

A Talented Dancer Takes Her Final Leap

Black Hills Weekly Pioneer, May 5, 1877.
Black Hills Weekly Times, December 4, 1877, and January 20, 1878.
Deadwood Pioneer-Times, December 8, 1877, and December 31, 1877.
Koller, Joe. "Kitty Leroy Dressed for Death When Murdered in 1877." *Rapid City Journal*, February 12, 1949.
Swisher, Kaija. "The Legend of Kitty LeRoy." *Black Hills Pioneer* (Spearfish, SD), September 4, 2015 (part 1), and September 11, 2015, (part 2).

The Gem's Kitty Clyde Murdered; Killer Then Shoots Himself

Custer Weekly Chronicle, November 10, 1883.
Daily Deadwood Pioneer-Times, November 6, 1883.
Deadwood Pioneer-Times, November 7, 1883.

A Gem Prostitute and a Knife

Daily Deadwood Pioneer-Times, May 3 and 6, 1884.
Deadwood Pioneer-Times, May 1, 1884.

Banjo Dick Shoots Shaughnessy at the Bella Union

Black Hills Champion, July 30, 1877.
Deadwood Pioneer-Times, July 27, 1877.
Rapid City Journal, September 21, 1924.
Yankton Press and Union and Dakotan, August 9, 1877.

The Unsolved Murder of Billy Bird

Black Hills Weekly Times, July 9, 1881.
Deadwood Pioneer-Times, July 19, 1881, and August 12, 1881.

Mr. Tuttle Killed in Treasure Gulch

Daily Deadwood Pioneer-Times, November 7, 1917.
Deadwood Pioneer-Times, September 5, 1877.

A Spoiled Teen and a Bad Temper

Cleveland Leader, October 27, 1882.
Daily Deadwood Pioneer-Times, November 14 and 21, 1882.
St. Louis Post-Dispatch, November 7, 1882.
Yankton Press and Dakotan, December 19, 1882.

Chief Two Sticks Hanged

Argus-Leader, December 11 and 25, 1894.
Guthrie Daily Leader, December 30, 1894.
Perry Chief, December 30, 1894.

Emma Stone Bludgeoned in Her Sleep

Argus-Leader, July 14, 1897.
Canton Farmers Leader, May 28, 1897.
Daily Deadwood Pioneer-Times, July 15, 1897.
Deadwood Evening Independent, July 14, 1897.
Hot Springs Weekly Star, July 16, 1897.
Queen City Mail, July 21, 1897.
Weekly Pioneer-Times, July 15, 1897.

The Death of China Doll

Deadwood Pioneer-Times, December 3 and 4, 1877.
Koller, Joe. "Yellow Dolls Murder Is Still a Mystery." *Rapid City Journal*, August 30, 1949.
St. Louis Globe-Democrat, December 6, 1877.

Deadwood Doctor Beaten

Black Hills Weekly Times, May 11 and 18, 1889.
Deadwood Pioneer-Times, May 9, 11 and 12, 1889.

The $220 Murder

Deadwood Pioneer-Times, May 6, 1878.
Leavenworth Press, May 16 and 30, 1878.
Public Ledger, May 10, 1878.

A Prank Goes Awry

Black Hills Weekly Times, August 6, 1892.
Deadwood Pioneer-Times, July 31, 1892, and April 30, 1878.

A Game of Cards Leads to Murder

Daily Deadwood Pioneer-Times, March 24, 1892.
Lincoln Nebraska State Journal, March 29, 1892.
Weekly Pioneer-Times, June 20 and 22, 1905.

Killed Over a Secret

Black Hills Weekly Pioneer, February 21, 1880.
Daily Deadwood Pioneer-Times, September 12, 1878; November 23 and 24, 1878; November 28, 1878.
Deadwood Pioneer-Times, September 11 and 12, 1878; November 8 and 25, 1878.

Deseret News, December 4, 1878.
New York Times, November 25, 1878.
Yankton Press and Dakotan, November 27, 1878.

Mistaken Identity and the Death of Bummer Dan

Deadwood Pioneer-Times, March 23, 1952.
Weekly Pioneer-Times, April 17, 1919, and July 2, 1931.

Midnight Murder in Deadwood

Daily Deadwood Pioneer-Times, May 9, 1909, and November 27, 1909.
Weekly Pioneer-Times, November 25, 1909.
Weekly Pioneer Times Mining Review, May 13, 1909.

Double Murder and Suicide

Lead Daily Call, August 24, 1939.
Rapid City Journal, August 23, 24 and 25, 1939.

A Woman, a Temper and a Six-Shooter Don't Mix!

Daily Deadwood Pioneer-Times, October 11 and 16, 1878.
Deadwood Pioneer-Times, July 30, 1878.

The Murder of California Joe

Bismarck Weekly Tribune, January 26, 1876, and April 5, 1876.
Chicago Weekly Post and Mail, January 27, 1876.
Independent-Record, November 17, 1876.
New York Daily Herald, November 5, 1876.
Rosa, Joseph G. "California Joe." *True West Magazine*, December 16, 2020. https://truewestmagazine.com.
Weekly Star, September 20, 1876.

The Unsolved Murder of Preacher Smith

Bullock, Captain Seth. "Historical Sketch of Death and Burial of Preacher Smith." *Daily Deadwood Pioneer-Times*, August 21, 1914.

Deadwood Pioneer-Times. "White Man May Have Killed Preacher Smith, Club Says." November 28, 1972.

Dead Man's Hand

Black Hills Weekly Pioneer, June 8, 1876.

California Democrat, July 19, 1877.

Daily Deadwood Pioneer-Times, September 29, 1891.

Deadwood Pioneer-Times, July 31, 1954, and June 8, 1876.

Democratic Leader, August 15 and 31, 1876.

Hamilton Spectator, October 1, 1886.

Kansas City Journal, August 22, 1876.

Weekly Pioneer-Times, September 10, 1903.

Western Spirit, September 1, 1876.

2. MAYHEM

Deadwood's Chinatown

Advocate-Messenger, March 30, 2005.

Weekly Pioneer-Times, November 21, 1940.

Suicide at the Fairmont Hotel

Sioux City Journal, September 2, 1907.

Weekly Pioneer-Times, September 5, 1907.

Sam Bass Gang

Black Hills Pioneer, July 9, 2013.

Daily Deadwood Pioneer-Times, July 28, 1881.

Lewallen, Ryan. "Slaughter's Golden Stage Line." This Week in Wyoming History, March 27, 2019.

The Curry Gang

Daily Deadwood Pioneer-Times, July 2, 1897; April 2, 1898; and March 1, 1900.
Weekly Pioneer-Times, July 23, 1903.

Homestake Pay Train Derailed

Deadwood Pioneer-Times, October 13 and 20, 1888.

Cayuse Bill and the Hidden Bullion in Deadwood's Beecher's Bluff

Black Hills Weekly Pioneer, March 26, 1881, and December 11, 1880.

The Great Fire of 1879

Black Hills Weekly Pioneer, December 6, 1879.
Daily Deadwood Pioneer-Times, November 19 and 20, 1879.

A Streaker in Deadwood?

Black Hills Weekly Pioneer, March 13, 1880.

The Demi-Blondes of Deadwood

Daily Deadwood Pioneer-Times, July 14, 1880.
Deadwood Pioneer-Times, June 18, 1879; September 26, 1879; and December 6, 1889.
Weekly Pioneer-Times, August 3, 1939.

Prohibition in Deadwood

Daily Deadwood Pioneer-Times, November 1, 1916; January 16, 1920; and June 12, 1920.
Deadwood Pioneer-Times, September 29, 1889.
Weekly Pioneer-Times, December 23, 1920.

The Popular Gem Variety Theatre

Daily Deadwood Pioneer-Times, December 31, 1879.
Deadwood Pioneer-Times, October 5, 1879.

Soiled Doves, Houses of Ill Repute and Dance Hall Girls

Black Hills Weekly Journal, January 16, 1914.
Black Hills Weekly Times, October 11, 1890, and November 22, 1890.
Daily Deadwood Pioneer-Times, November 28, 1890, and May 19, 1920.
Weekly Pioneer-Times, May 9, 1929.

The Wildest Mayhem Maker of Deadwood, Calamity Jane

Daily Deadwood Pioneer-Times, June 29, 1928.
Deadwood Pioneer-Times, July 26, 1953; August 3, 1953; August 1, 1948; and July 31, 1954.
Illustrated American. "Interview with Calamity Jane." Vol. 19, no. 316 (March 7, 1896).
San Francisco Call and Post, November 18, 1896.
Weekly Pioneer-Times, September 10, 1903.

BIBLIOGRAPHY

Websites

Ancestry. https://www.ancestry.com.
Find a Grave. https://www.findagrave.com.
HistoryLink.org. https://www.historylink.org.
Legends of America. https://www.legendsofamerica.com.
Library of Congress. http://www.loc.gov.
True West. https://www.truewestmagazine.com
Wikimedia. https://www.wikimedia.org.

Books and Features

Bell, Bob Boze. "Bad Day at Round Rock," *True West*, June 1, 2010. https://truewestmagazine.com.

Brown, Jesse, and A.M. Willard. *The Black Hills Trails: A History of the Struggles of the Pioneers in the Winning of the Black Hills.* Rapid City Journal Company, 1924.

Bryant, Jerry, and Bill Markley. "Death of Deadwood's China Doll." HistoryNet.com, June 20, 2017. https://www.historynet.com.

Coroner's Report on Albert Ellis (Swearengen). Denver Public Library Special Collections, item WH842. Courtesy of reference librarian Alex Hernandez.

Hernandez, Alejandro. "Deadwood's Despicable Mack Daddy Al Swearengen: The Brothel Owner Abused 'Soiled Doves' in Dakota Before Karma Came Calling in Denver." HistoryNet.com, January 5, 2024.

Historic Round Rock Collection. "The Story of Sam Bass." https://www.roundrocktexas.gov.

Illustrated American. "Interview with Calamity Jane." Vol. 19, no. 316 (March 7, 1896).

Lewallen, Ryan. "Slaughter's Golden Stage Line." This Week in Wyoming History, March 27, 2019.

Rosa, Joseph G. "California Joe," *True West*, December 16, 2020. https://truewestmagazine.com.

Swisher, Kaija. "The Legend of Kitty LeRoy." *Black Hills Pioneer*, September 4, 2015 (part 1), and September 11, 2015 (part 2).

Newspapers

Argus Leader (Sioux Falls, SD)
December 9, 1895
January 10, 1920
September 7, 1926

Bismarck Weekly Tribune (Bismarck, ND)
January 26, 1876
April 5, 1876

Black Hills Daily Times (Deadwood, SD)
April 12–13, 1877
April 17, 1877
September 5–6, 1877
November 28, 1877
December 3, 4 and 8, 1877
February 8 and 18, 1878
February 28, 1878
December 8, 1878
February 3, 1879
November 4, 15 and 22, 1879
December 24, 1879
January 16, 1880
February 17, 18 and 28, 1880
March 2 and 4, 1880
May 25, 1880
April 12 and 29, 1881

May 12, 1881
July 7, 1881
July 19, 1881
August 13, 1881
February 13–14, 1883
October 12, 1883
August 26 and 29, 1885
November 22, 1885
March 30, 1886
August 4, 1888
October 20, 1888
February 17, 1889
May 11, 1889
December 6, 1889
September 26, 1890
March 24, 1892
July 31, 1892
May 29, 1894
October 5, 1895
September 10, 11, 12, 16 and 25, 1926
May 11, 1927
February 3, 1928

Black Hills News-Letter and Mining Reporter (Deadwood, SD)
December 30, 1878

Black Hills Weekly Journal (Rapid City, SD)
May 29, 1880

Black Hills Weekly Pioneer Times (Deadwood, SD)
February 21, 1880
April 14, 17 and 21, 1880
March 6, 1930

Black Hills Weekly Times (Deadwood, SD)
July 15, 1876
August 5, 1876
November 25, 1876
August 26, 1877

December 4, 1877
December 23, 1877
April 4, 1878
April 29, 1878
January 31, 1880
March 13, 1880
April 17, 1880
November 13, 1880
October 30, 1880
July 5, 1881
July 23, 1881
August 29, 1885
September 18, 1888
May 10–18, 1889
November 22, 1890
April 16, 1892
June 22, 1905
February 8, 1930
February 27, 1930
June 8, 1976
April 16, 1980

Chase County Leader (Cottonwood Falls, KS)
June 26, 1884

Chicago Tribune (Chicago, IL)
June 17, 1880

Cincinnati Enquirer (Cincinnati, OH)
February 9, 1878

Daily Deadwood Pioneer Times (Deadwood, SD)
July 27, 1877
September 19–25, 1878
October 30, 1878
November 23, 1878
January 29, 1879
February 19, 1880

March 24, 1881
November 30, 1881
January 1, 1882
July 25–27, 1882
September 18, 1883
October 12, 1883
November 6, 1883
November 12–20, 1883
April 3 and 4, 1884
May 6, 1884
September 25, 1885
February 23, 1889
January 11, 1890
March 24, 1892
December 20, 1894
July 5, 1899
February 27, 1901
September 5, 1903
February 21, 1905
July 22, 1905
August 31, 1905
December 8, 1906
October 2, 1908
April 21, 1912
July 18, 1913
March 28, 1920
April 8, 1923
September 10–14, 1926
September 25, 1926
October 29, 1927
April 23, 1930
October 13, 1932

Daily Sentinel (Grand Junction, CO)
May 25, 1970

Dakota Chief (Gann Valley, SD)
June 29, 1905

Deadwood Evening Independent (Deadwood, SD)
December 6, 1895

Deadwood Independent (Deadwood, SD)
July 14, 1897

Deadwood Weekly Pioneer Times (Deadwood, SD)
June 8, 1876
April 21, 1877
August 21, 1878
November 10 and 22, 1878
February 13–15, 1880
March 13, 1880
November 26, 1882
December 7, 14 and 16, 1882
February 13, 1885
February 9, 1893
August 5, 1893
November 23, 1893
March 8–15, 1894
September 13, 1894
December 5, 1895
June 17, 1897
July 15, 1897
March 24, 1898
November 7, 1901
March 16, 1905
June 1 and 8, 1905
July 27, 1905
September 5, 1908
August 13, 1908
November 8, 1913
December 12 and 24, 1919
May 5, 1921
May 19, 1921
August 18, 1921
October 27, 1921
November 3, 1921
December 5, 1922

June 9, 1927
December 8, 1927
May 9, 1929
November 9, 1930
July 2, 1931
December 17, 1931
July 9, 1936
February 10, 1938
August 24, 1939
November 21, 1940
July 29, 1960
July 25, 1969

Democrat Leader (Cheyenne, WY)
July 22, 1876
April 30, 1878
February 14, 1883

Des Moines Register (Des Moines, IA)
October 2, 1904

Helena Independent (Helena, MT)
June 11, 1896

Jackson's Hole Courier (Jackson, WY)
April 27, 1950

Kansas City Star (Kansas, MS)
April 22, 1923

Kenosha News (Kenosha, WI)
February 8, 1928

Lead Call (Lead, SD)
April 18, 1901
April 14, 1906
December 8, 1919
September 13, 1926
May 23, 1931
January 7, 1935

Livingston County Daily Press and Argus (Howell, MI)
February 4, 1876

Madison Daily Leader (Madison, SD)
December 13, 1919
January 28, 1920
March 27, 1920

Montgomery Advertiser (Montgomery, AL)
August 27, 1884

Rapid City Journal (Rapid City, SD)
August 23–25, 1939

Sioux City Journal (Sioux City, IA)
February 22, 1883
September 2, 1907
March 5, 1910

Springfield Weekly Patriot (Springfield, MO)
May 9, 1878

St. Louis Globe-Democrat (St. Louis, MO)
August 20, 1876
December 6, 1877

Sturgis Advertiser (Sturgis, SD)
June 6, 1888

Sun Journal (Lewiston, ID)
March 14, 1923

Weekly Kansas City Star (Kansas City, MO)
May 29, 1935

Weekly Pioneer Times Mining Review (Deadwood, SD)
July 17, 1913

Wichita Star (Wichita, KS)
July 17, 1890

Yankton Press & Dakotan (Yankton, SD)
August 23, 1877
December 10, 1877
June 19, 1878

Additional Deadwood Resources

Deadwood History Inc. includes:

Adams Museum
54 Sherman Street
Deadwood, SD 57732
(605) 578 1714

The Brothel Deadwood
610 Main Street
Deadwood, SD 57732
(605) 559 0231

Days of '76 Museum
18 Seventy-Six Drive
Deadwood, SD 57732
(605) 578 1657

Historic Adams House
22 Van Buren Street
Deadwood, SD 57732
(605) 578 3724

Homestake Adams Research and Cultural Center
150 Sherman Street
Deadwood, SD 57732
(605) 722 4800

Also visit:

Mount Moriah Cemetery
2 Mount Moriah Road
Deadwood, SD 57732
(605) 578 2600

For an excellent look into the life and times of the farmers and pioneers from the old days, visit the New Agricultural Museum, Buggy Museum and Historical House at 102 East Johnson Avenue, Stockholm, South Dakota, 57264. The museum, part of the Grant County Historical Society, is open on Saturdays from May through September. Visit https://www.grantcountysdmuseums.org.

INDEX

L

M

N

O

P

R

S

W

Y

ABOUT THE AUTHOR

Originally from Ithaca, New York, Deborah Cuyle loves everything about the history of America's cities—large or small. Her other passions include volunteering at her local historical society, rescuing animals, exploring museums, rock hunting and horses. Deadwood and the Black Hills are on the list of her top ten favorite places to enjoy, and she hopes to live there someday!

Also by Deborah Cuyle

Ghostly Tales of Coeur d'Alene (ID)

Ghostly Tales of Snohomish (WA)

Ghostly Tales of the Pacific Northwest (OR, WA and BC)

Ghosts and Legends of Northeast South Dakota (SD)

Ghosts and Legends of Spokane (WA)

Ghosts of Coeur d'Alene and the Silver Valley (ID)

Ghosts of Leavenworth and the Cascade Foothills (WA)

Haunted Eastern Washington (WA)

Haunted Everett (WA)

Haunted Snohomish (WA)

Haunted Southwest Montana (MT)

Images of Cannon Beach (OR)

Kidding Around Portland (OR)

Murder and Mayhem in Coeur d'Alene and the Silver Valley (ID)

Murder and Mayhem in Spokane (WA)

The 1910 Wellington Disaster (WA)

Wicked Coeur d'Alene (ID)

Wicked Spokane (WA)